NIEL LIBESKIND

±

BETWEEN ZERO AND INFINITY

SELECTED PROJECTS IN ARCHITECTURE

∞

To the loving memory of my mother Dora and my father-in-law David
Lewis, both of whom sadly, died during the preparation of this book.

2

ACKNOWLEDGEMENTS

Designed by Mark Tweed, Lori Barnett, and Craig Minor, at Cranbrook Academy of Art, under the direction of Katherine McCoy, Co-chairman of the Department of Design. Daniel Libeskind provided the critical foundation for the development of the format.

Special appreciation is extended to the following: Ben Nicholson, Fumio Hatano and Sripong Thanapura, and for technical assistance to Katsuhiko Muramoto, Steven Rost and Jim Abbott.

Cover design: Lori Barnett

First published in the United States of America in 1981 by
Rizzoli International Publications, Inc.
712 Fifth Avenue, New York, NY 10019   *387-3400*

ISBN: 0 – 8478 – 0412 – 7
LC: 81 – 51635

Printed and bound in the U.S.A.

DANIEL LIBESKIND

BETWEEN ZERO AND INFINITY

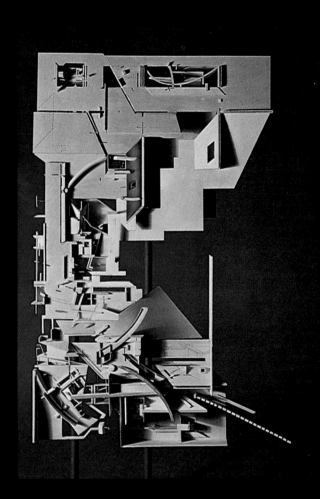

DANIEL LIBESKIND

Daniel Libeskind heads the Department of Architecture at the Cranbrook Academy of Art. Born in 1946 in Poland, he first studied music
in Lodz and continued his musical education through the
America-Israel Cultural Foundation Fellowship in Israel. On moving
to America in 1960, he became interested in architecture via his involvement in mathematics and painting.

He studied at the Cooper Union School of Architecture in New York
where he received a Bachelor of Architecture, **summa cum laude.** He
gained his Master of Arts Degree in the History and Theory of Architecture from the School of Comparative Studies, Essex University,
England with a dissertation on the problem of 'Imagination and
Space'.

He has taught at the Universities of Toronto and Kentucky,
Polytechnic of Central London, and Architectural Association in
London from 1975-1977. Since 1978, he has been architect-in-
residence at the Cranbrook Academy of Art.

He has worked with architectural firms in New York, Den Haag and
Toronto, and has lectured extensively throughout Europe, Scandina-
via and North America.

He has participated in exhibitions in New York's Museum of Modern
Art, Art Net (London) and the Cranbrook Museum.

Most recently, he has exhibited his work in Helsinki, London, New
York, Houston, Stockholm and Zurich.

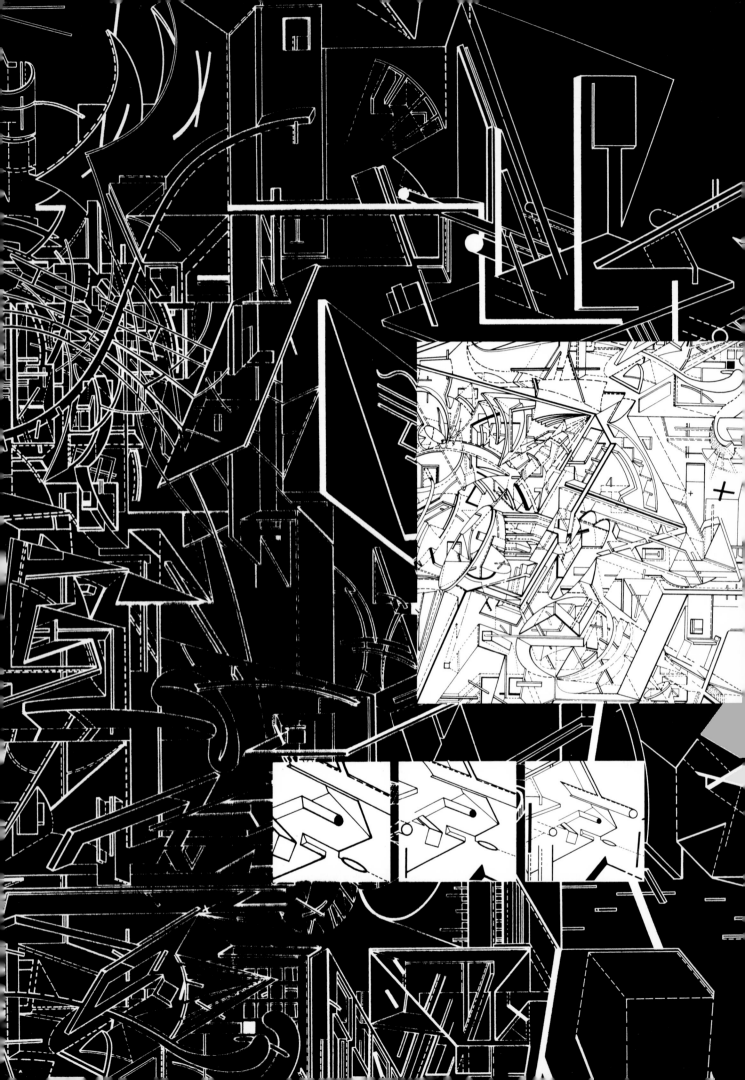

METAL SPIKES STAR CAPPED

I.   Somewhere or other there is written an American short story called "Paul's Case". The story begins with the awakening on a winter morning of a boy named Paul. He goes over to his bedroom window and stares outward. Dawn is just beginning and it is just starting to snow. Paul takes a wood chair and places it by the window so that he can sit in the chair and watch the snow flakes thicken. He spends the whole day just looking out the window at the falling snow which begins to fill the sky making it whiter and thicker. The snow continously, steadily falls, and Paul continuously, steadily watches the falling snow. In the last paragraph of the story the snow has crossed over, that is the snow begins to fall within the head, mind, and soul of Paul, it begins softly to fill his head, gently at first, and soon it entirely fills the inside of Paul. So it ends when he is filled with a density of white opacities.

II.   Sometime during the 14th Century in Venice, the Doge wished to build a tower taller than any other tower ever built in Venice so that he could be closer to the heavens. He employed the best stone masons available in Venice and he inported the finest stone for the construction of the tower. The tower was halfway built up when a condition was noticed. That is the tower began to to sink into the earth. This alarmed the Doge, he ordered that the construction be accelerated. But as more stones were added the tower continued to sink. When the tower was finally completed, the top of the tower was on the exact level of the surface of the earth. The Venetians were pleased, for their Doge when standing at the top of the tower was at their level, the earth plane level. Even the Doge was pleased, although he was no closer the heavens, his feet were at least closer to the earth, and being a practical Venetian this fact gave him pleasure.

III.   Somehow there is located at the bottom of South America an old 17th Century structure which houses pre-historic armadillos. These armadillos are of a larger size than our present day ones. There are I believe seven or eight. Presently it is tranquil in that space, this has not always been so. In the middle of the 18th Century some things were noticed. In short there was a time when the seven enclosed armadillos began to grow, imperceptibly at first. The custodian thought that there were some changes going on. So he began to measure the fixed specimens, each day they did grow a bit. The officials began to worry, for if this situation continued they would be forced to remove one or two or possibly all of the armadillos. They were simply at a loss as to what to do. As it happened there was repair work going on within the building. One day a carpenter drove a star headed metal spike into the wall of the structure. On that day the armadillos failed to grow. But the next day they continued to do so. It was reasoned that perhaps if a star headed metal spike was driven each day into the internal enclosing walls of the building that growth could be prevented. So each day a spike was driven into the wall. The armadillos did not grow. Finally one day the entire surface of the enclosing walls was filled with metal stars and a strange condition occured. The wall surfaces not covered by the metal star heads began to bleed, but only the spaces between the star heads bled. Then the blood dried and from that day on no more growth could be detected. The officials then decided to plaster over the metal stars and dried blood.

Today when there, one can tap the plaster walls and hear soft metallic echoes, and if one puts one's ear close to the plaster surface, one can even imagine hearing the flow of liquid.

* dedicated to Lev

Daniel Libeskind knows something of the above. He has plunged his hand up into the heavens and has caught some stars and at the moment of his contact the stars have turned to metal and have achieved weight and our universe has turned to the density of a pewter reflecting a light unseen before.

John Hejduk
Architect
New York, January 1981

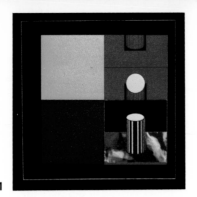

1.1

8 New York 1969

1.2

1.3

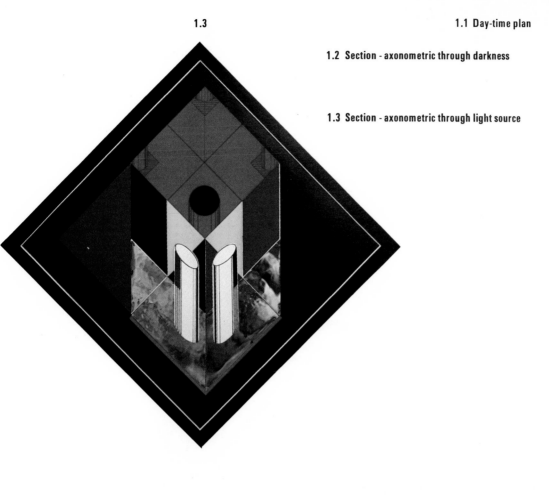

1.2 Section - axonometric through darkness

1.3 Section - axonometric through light source   New York 1969 **9**

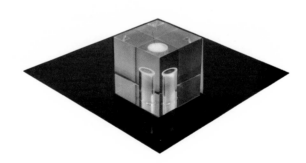

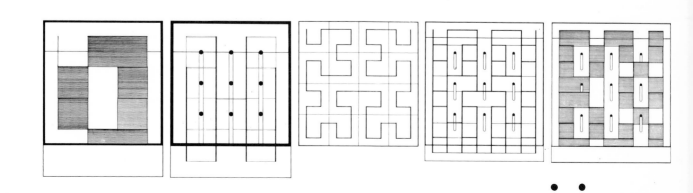

1

1.4

1.5

1.5 Nighttime plan

1.4 Site   **1.6 Model**

1.6

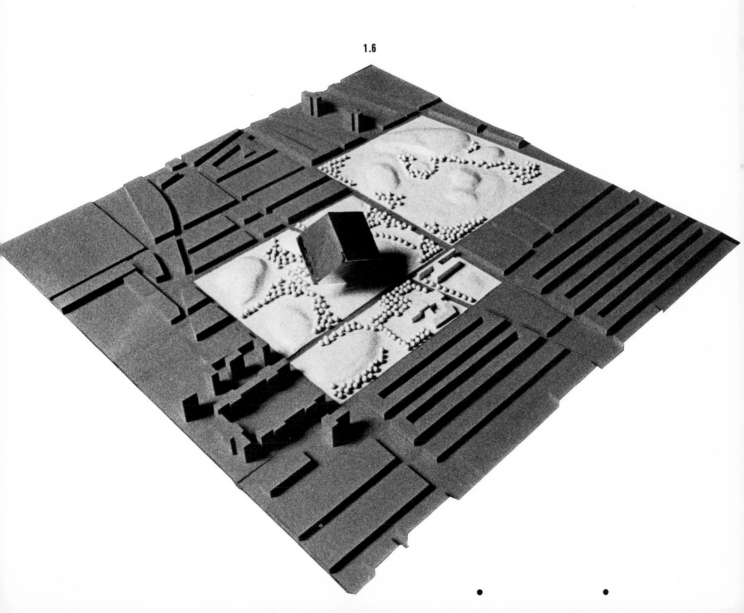

1

1.7

New York 1969

1.8

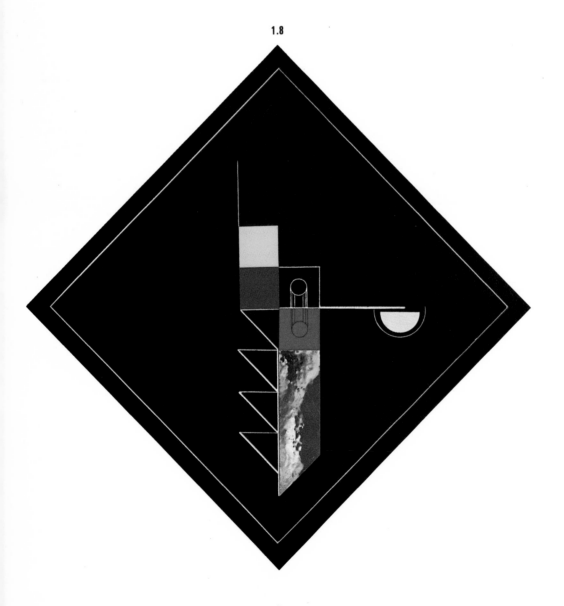

1.7 Reappearance

1.8 Clearing

1.9 Model

1.9

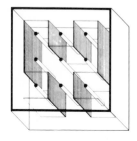

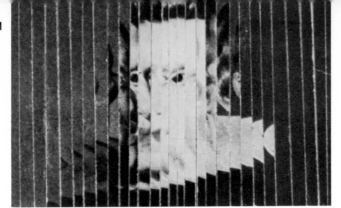

2.1

2.2

2.3

2.4

3.1

3 COLLAGE INSCAPES

New York 1969 **17**

3.2
3.3

4 COLLAGE ARCHITECTURE

4.1

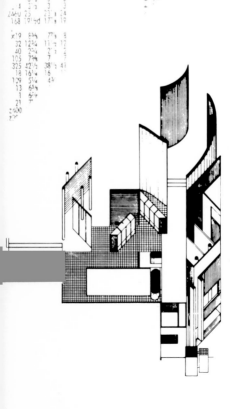

continued   Page 14

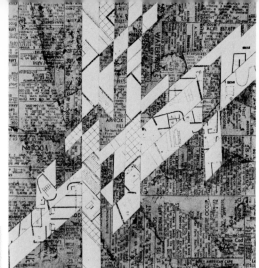

4.2 Collage section

4.3 Collage section

4.1 Model: House with detached profiles

4.2

4.3

'Are you laughing again? Go ahead, laugh, but I still won't say that my belly is full when I'm hungry; I still won't content myself with a compromise, with an infinitely recurring zero just because it is allowed to recur by some law, just because it's there. I don't accept as the crowning of my dreams a big building for the poor, with apartments leased for one thousand years and a dentist's sign outside in case of emergency.'

Fyodor Dostoyevsky
'Notes From Underground'

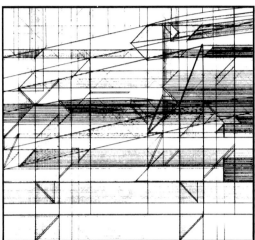

4.4

4

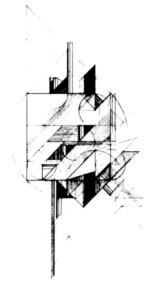

4.6

4

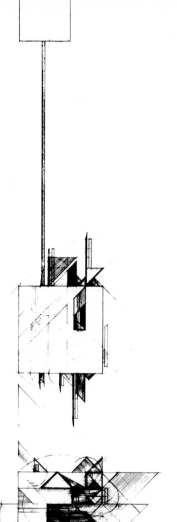

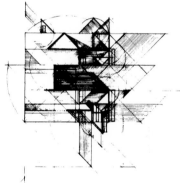

4.6a

4

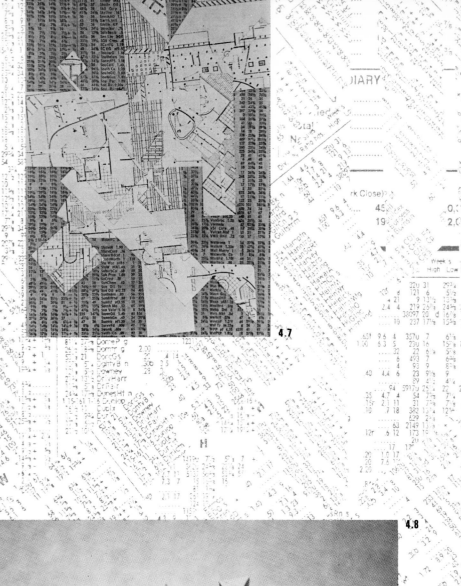

4.7

4.8

4.8a

4.8b

4.7 Collage plan

4.8 Model: House with detached profiles II

4.9 Collage plan

4.9

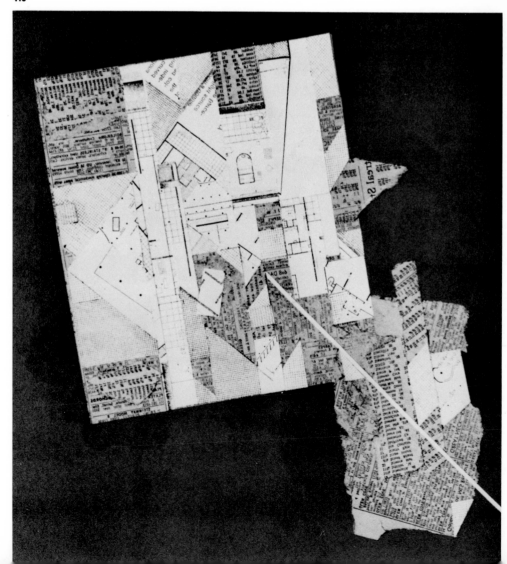

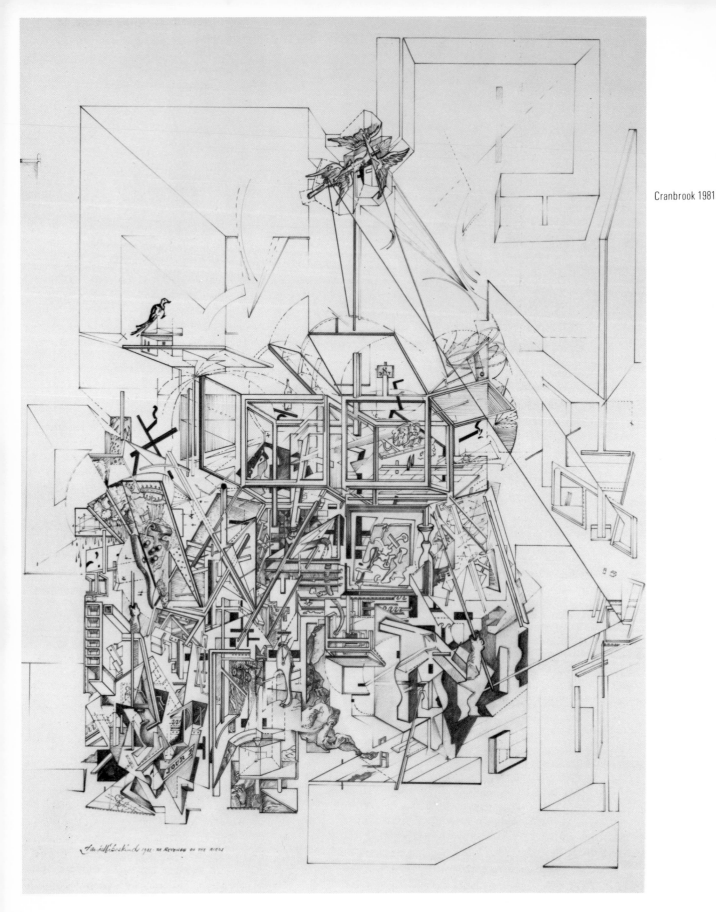

Revenge of the Birds

SYMBOL AND INTERPRETATION

Architecture and architectural education reflect more accurately perhaps than any of the other arts, the order of society, the ideology of formal configuration and the limits beyond which forms become unacceptable and are simply considered as irrelevant and disorderly. This condition seems to arise from the close historical collaboration which exists between the reality of building, its symbolic milieu and the reciprocal consequences of their mutual transposition.

I do not intend to give here a philosophical or historically detailed analysis which would account for the profound changes in our contemporary form of community and its architecture. However, I do feel that if one is to gain a deeper understanding of our everyday landscape, one must look anew on the situated meaning and the meaning of our situation in architecture. Such an interpretation should attempt to understand the progress and significance of the kind of reason and objectification immanent to the Age of Representation. In our search for a more profound understanding of the implications of building and dwelling, we should examine the full genealogy of culture, extending from the manifest political, economic and social dimensions to their more obscure ontological sources. We should look at the correlations which exist today between the structure of life and its embodiments in the world; between desire and possession; between freedom and necessity; between utopia and home-coming.

Architecture has always been concerned with the problem of the creation of order; with structuring that which is to occupy the central arena of interest in the theatre of reality, and that which is to be relegated to the margins. It is common in schools of architecture to be taught that some structures and designs are natural, proper and orderly, in short representative of the world; and that others, especially those which contain an element of fantasy, a different kind of reasoning, or seem irreverent to the given system of production are unacceptable and unnatural. We might enquire whence this moral judgement arises and in whose interest it is perpetuated; why it is, for example, that certain types of forms, materials, programs and social directives are habitually and automatically utilized. Perhaps it is these deeply ingrained habits and their corresponding cliches which form in history the armature of the Absolute.

An astounding phenomenon occurs when a sudden virus seems to sweep across an entire architectural culture, beginning locally and spreading rapidly through the schools and the profession. It is a time when certain forms are paralyzed by a tacit refusal to grant them 'right' and is a symptom of the unendurability of any kind of objective order. A mere fifty years ago, an enthusiastic generation, believing itself to be the harbinger of a true and new reality, attempted a radical overthrow of what it considered an old and empty order. However, what was condemned and rejected then has once again become a cherished and plausible alternative. This cyclical alternation between order and disorder reflects a change in appearances only, and conceals those very premises whose consequences its harshest critics would seek to denounce today. The vicious circularity of styles testifies to the oblivion of foundations amidst the frantic excess of measuring and calculating objects.

What is interesting in all of this is not the actual outward changes in buildings and their corresponding polemics, but the fact that a particular set of configurations and geometries seen as naturally representative can become in a short time unnatural and morally taboo. The problem of order in architecture, as elsewhere, is not merely a formal problem but one which is linked to a moral and ethical view of society; so too the handling of disorder. The dream of a City of Man where moral duty would be linked to civic obedience via the notion of 'space' is itself a dimension of the history of architecture deeply rooted in an authoritarian tradition of constraint.

Disorder, the arbitrary, born from the delirium of order pushed beyond its limits, by a strange paradox, discovers its own logic; a structure which like an inaccessible and secret truth has been prefigured in the alluring depths of chaos. When we deploy the arbitrary, we confront necessity - our own and the world's. Already at the threshold of our century, two philosophical masters perceived the implications and the dilemma of this nihilating freedom: Kierkegaard and Dostoevsky. In the words of Kierkegaard: 'The whole truth lies in arbitrariness', and in those of Dostoevsky: 'Twice two makes four is nothing but a piece of impudence...a farcical, dressed-up fellow who stands across your path with arms akimbo and spits at you.' After all, if twice two makes five is also possible, then humanity no longer limits freedom, but is limited and determined by it.

In the twilight zone where Order is eclipsed; where at the margins of experience, symbolic structures can no longer domesticate perception; where evaluations, opinions and attitudes replace the certainty of shared conviction - order becomes an ironic sign inverting the relation between fiction and reality. Fictions of an ideal world with their pretended universality reduce the full implication of spatiality to a prior notion of a homogeneous and empty datum ready for quantification.

For over two centuries now, we have been witness to a gradual reduction and functionalization of both architecture and architectural education. This systematization, already explicitly institutionalized by Durand at the Ecole Polytechnique, at the beginning of the 19th Century, has continued to exert an insidious if not apparent influence to this day. To treat architecture and its teaching as a solving operation of a problem 'X' is akin to treating reality as if it were destined to wind up on the operating table. That fateful and remarkable encounter between the 'sewing machine and the umbrella on the operating table' has given birth to a whole bestiary of creatures and monsters - and not only in the mind. (The use of the word monster in this context refers to its etymology, that is, portentous revelation or demonstration). The process whereby the making of architecture comes to resemble a laboratory experiment reflects the general secularization of culture, whose symptoms include the relativization of meaning, the devaluation of tradition and the virulent attack on all forms of symbolic, emblematic and mythical experience.

The transformation of meaning through formalization of lived-experience is exemplified in our contemporary concepts of space and time. The ever increasing fragmentation and dispersal of human knowledge is evident in the multitude of specialized disciplines. We have today a space/time which belongs to historians, biologists, physicists, sociologists, psychologists and hosts of others; competing concepts and schools which cannot be reconciled in any comprehensive framework of understanding. These emptied forms of time, space, self and the world have in common the presupposition of an objective, neutral and detached knowledge; a knowledge which can be attained only through specialization and sophisticated acts of reason whose achievement is the guarding talisman of modernity. But this objective conditioning by rules, regulations, taboos and accepted codes of orderly design (what is called taste, propriety, context, decorum, relying on the long tradition of enforcing cues of order) is not something that we must take for granted or consider as if it were eternally true. The 'laws' of Architecture and its dogmatics are not inscribed in the lineaments of Solomon's Temple, nor in the eternal properties of the cube, nor in some ideal geometry of phenomena. These are all constructions based on the axiomatic of systems which can be exhaustively defined. But in the making of architecture there can be no question of defining its objectives by any system of laws which would seek to reconstruct our experiences anew. This tendency to consider one of the properties of Architecture (property of objects) as Architecture itself leads only to a gross presumption. The attempt to manipulate and reify the whole of human reality with the intention of appropriating it as if it were an object, forgets in the process that the ordering of means themselves can never disclose valid and authentic ends.

Those architectural exercises which model themselves after a scientific methodology and seem to appropriate reality-in-itself, as-it-is, are themselves only artificial means instituted on behalf of an often forgotten metaphysical quest. In representing the making of architecture as an autonomous activity (having more affinity to technique than science) this thinking intentionally narrows itself to a process of **data**-collecting operations. To build and think dwelling is reduced to an experimental 'set': testing, transforming and manipulating those phenomena which have been thoroughly purified of any opacity or contamination by a meaning not in its control. In fact the outcome of this process more often than not, is the generation of forms produced by the apparatus of 'research' itself, rather than authentic apprehension of phenomena. The building is thus a consequence of decisions permitted only under the preconstituted scope of definitions and may indeed be very different from the intentions and expectations of the operator himself. In the spectrum of abstraction ranging from the simple measuring instruments to cybernetic systems we witness the dissociation of personal vision from its archetypal and historical matrix. This dissociation manifests itself on one hand, in the depersonalized handling of 'ready-mades', and on the other in the world of private fantasies devoid of a public dimension.

This artificial thinking which is always a confrontation with the object-in-general, models itself on information theory, naturalistic science and behavioral conditioning in order to construct an ultimate process whose very artificiality requires (even if in a distant future) an automaton to fulfill it. In order to construct things on the basis of a few abstract indices or variables, this flattened and technicized thinking and making ignores the fundamental conditions, situations, and the site of its own manifestation. Ceasing to live fully at home in this world, it relinquishes the enigmatic encounter with things and places. With this kind of seeing, traffic lights come to mean more than the light of the stars and the measurment of space more than the life which animates and constitutes it. The presumption that space can be treated as a system of coordinates, an empty cage from which there is no recourse or escape, a quality reduced to a homogeneous quantative datum where everything is equal to itself, is a tautology without depth or horizon. It is a reflection of a false identity in which space itself really means nothing and yet is predestined for our own use.

This 'artificial paradise' appearing increasingly in our experience of everyday life, reveals the nightmare quality of a utopia - a no-where-land in which remembrance and consciousness will be soon considered as useless fragments in a topography of pure reason. In a space without hiding places where content is separable from location; where each thing stands isolated and exposed to Nothing: where the human face is no longer necessary for the existence of a 'space-in-itself', envelopment in Being comes to mean shelter in environment.

What B.F. Skinner has called the era 'beyond human dignity and freedom' has become a real possibility for us in architecture and planning. We too can become the technicians of the sublime and marvellous magic which can conjure away historical existence by the numbing use of cyphers and cybernetic techniques. But what is it that lies beyond freedom and dignity? Is it the world of a fully anesthetized behavior? Is it perhaps the world of Skinner himself and of a chain of anonymous collaborators engineering the final solution to the 'problem' of man? How will this future world, already around us in sketch form appear? Will it look like the laboratory whose apparatus provides the stoic regimen in which man (the technician) takes himself to be the one of the objects of his own manipulation? Or will it be indeed the final triumph of Utopia; a no place.

These questions are not merely hypothetical or rhetorical. They are questions which depict very real and contemporary paradoxes. One of the prerogatives of this wondering stance is the opportunity it affords us as students of architecture to unmask and deconstruct these situations, to examine our position vis-a-vis our own freedom and dignity. Technological order and planning, systems organization and simulation games; all these gambits and not infallible ones either, gimmicks which count as particular items in the temporal unfolding of reality. Through our examination, we have the inkling that this paraphernalia of gadgetry is not a historical accident but a symbol of the profound separation which veils all our encounters; a

'Eternally chained to only one single little fragment of the whole, Man himself grew to be only a fragment...Instead of imprinting humanity upon his nature, he becomes merely the imprint of his occupation.'

Friedrich Schiller
'On the Aesthetic Education of Man'

mask which testifies to the alienating split which rends our experience by opening it to the constant threat of falsehood.

In fact our questioning needs to go further. We can wonder whether the world has been created once and for all; whether our duty lies in reproducing according to the models of object, order and type, handed to us by a binding authority. We can take up seriously our own experience, that architecture (like man) is unfinishable and permanently deferred, that it has no nature, that its tradition is an event, a happening in which we are inextricably caught.

To simplify, we have today a conflict between two differing tendencies. One claims that the 'natural' development of Architecture depends on the appropriation and ultimate domination of technique, inevitably leading to the objectification and quantification - the consumption of the space of encounters. The other tendency sees Architecture as an autonomous and self-referential discipline, inventing its own tradition through mute monuments. However, there is an approach which is not as simple or clear to define as the above, but which attempts nevertheless to deal with the poetic complexity of Architecture in time. It seeks to explore the deeper order rooted not only in visible forms, but in the invisible and hidden sources which nourish culture itself, in its thought, art, literature, song and movement. It considers history and tradition as a body whose memories and dreams cannot be simply reconstructed. Such an approach does not wish to reduce the visible to a thought, and architecture to a mere construction. An orientation such as this admits in its methods and testifies in its intentions to the intensity of experience, to its 'opaque transparency', and by its deferred expectations continually calls its own presuppositions into question.

The work in the studio at Cranbrook attempts to deal with architecture in an analytic, interpretive, symbolic, non representational manner. We believe that nothing is ever fully figurative because a certain density clings to all our symbolic encounters, be they expressed in words or figures; cyphers or codes. Significance never fully exhausts its resources because there is always a residue left over which points to the correspondence or analogy which mediates the density of things and the ambiguity of meaning. Our point of departure therefore is never the abstract programming of an object but rather the search for valid objectives.

The ways of systematically objectifying architectural values, a conversion of objects into objects, is an effort to project experience as a process devoid of depth and concealment. But in whatever manner we represent architecture, be it as idea, matter, energy or the eternal recurrence of the same types, we must remember that objects appearing to us have already been revealed on a primordial and non-figurative level. There can be nothing fully figurative in the sense that meaning remains occluded in the symbols which convey it. If we understand architecture as having a symbolic nature, then we have already entered into a domain both more fundamental and original; a

realm where the decisions and interpretations of meaning are already historically underway.

The necessity of rigorous imagination and the project of discovering possible means of emancipation in architecture must be recognized as crucial, as the concrete sources of inspiration in progressively more advanced societies expire in institutionalized habits of thought and action. The poverty of the so called 'real world' must be unmasked as a form of a ruling ideology whose interests and ambitions do not necessarily coincide with our full existence and its aspirations. It has been pointed out more than once that good taste is only a form of acquired censorship. The awareness that pleasing, flattery and 'service to society' are often so many codes for techniques of deception, compels us to rethink the widely held belief that there is a pre-destined and correct expression assigned a priori to each form by the 'language of Architecture' itself, as if this 'language' belonged to the ceremonies and rituals themselves.

In order to release creative architectural interpretation from the grip of and the fidelity to the petty and circumstantial preoccupations of rhetoric, (form-for-form's-sake) and especially from the representational narration of the past, (historicism-ecclecticism) we are pursuing a projective poetics of architecture. We see in this phenomenology of space the polymorphic, shifting oneiric substance of Architecture - the interrogation which is the fragile and precise kernel of understanding and invention.

In the end, we are brought back to questioning the relation between signs and symbols. Can we say that the plastic meaning of architecture consists in an internal self-sustaining structure, and that this autonomy forms the hidden secret of space, so that finally it is in the splendour of the visible that its truth is revealed and exhausted? Or does the significance of architectural works and its affirming power lie in a movement of the truth-of-time as a whole, rising from the plastic-sensible as does lightning from thunder, abandoning the visible to the inertia and contingency of its own obscurity? Can visible form still carry the destiny of Architecture? In any case, forms are not yet dead and it is finally in the transfiguration of the concrete that we have access to that mystery of which forms and meanings give us only a provisional and portentous outline.

Daniel Libeskind

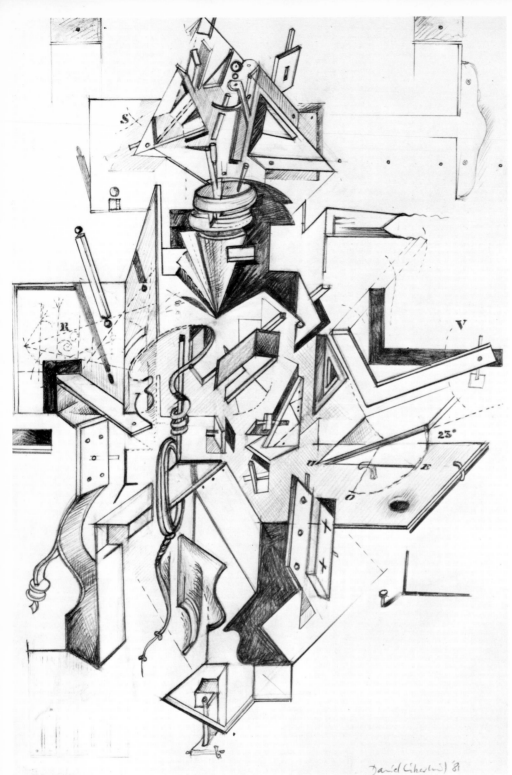

Cranbrook 1981

ARTIFICIAL ALLUREMENT

Cranbrook 1981

"AND IT CAN'T BE HELPED"

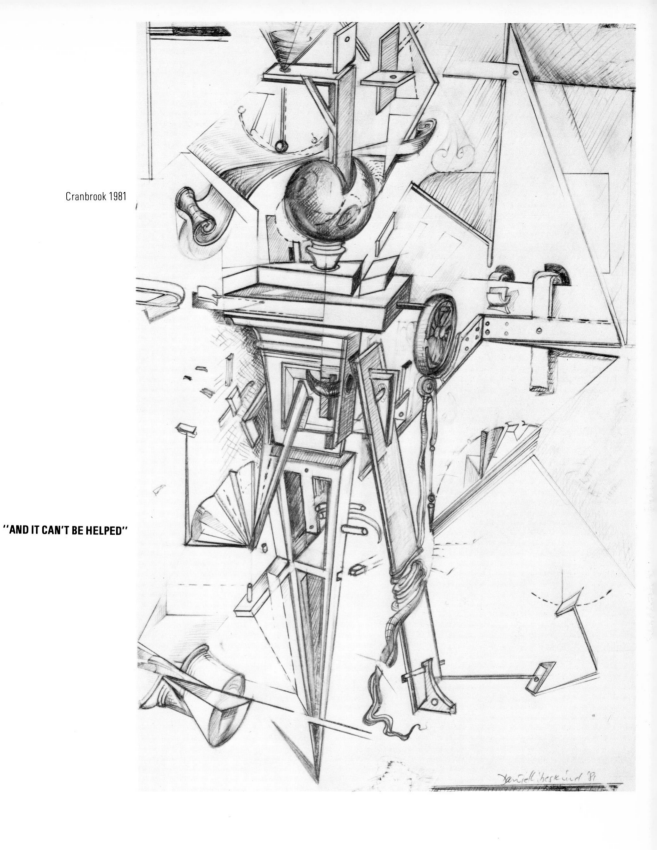

5.1

5

6 COLLAGE REBUS 1

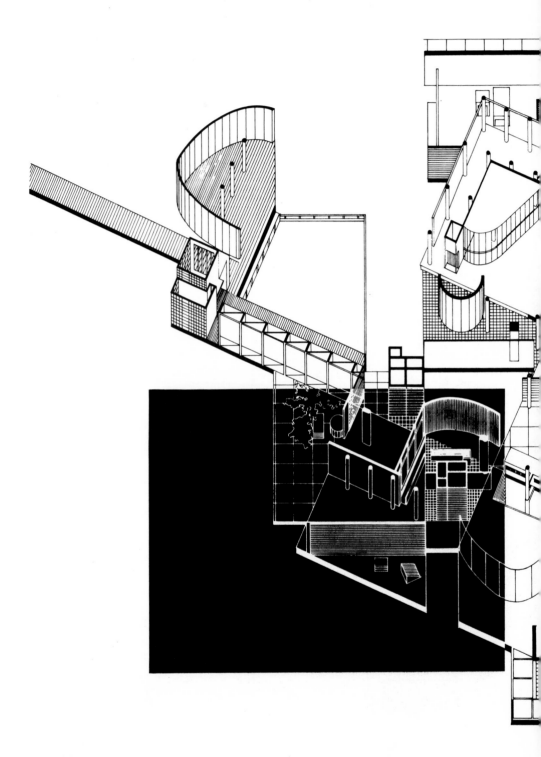

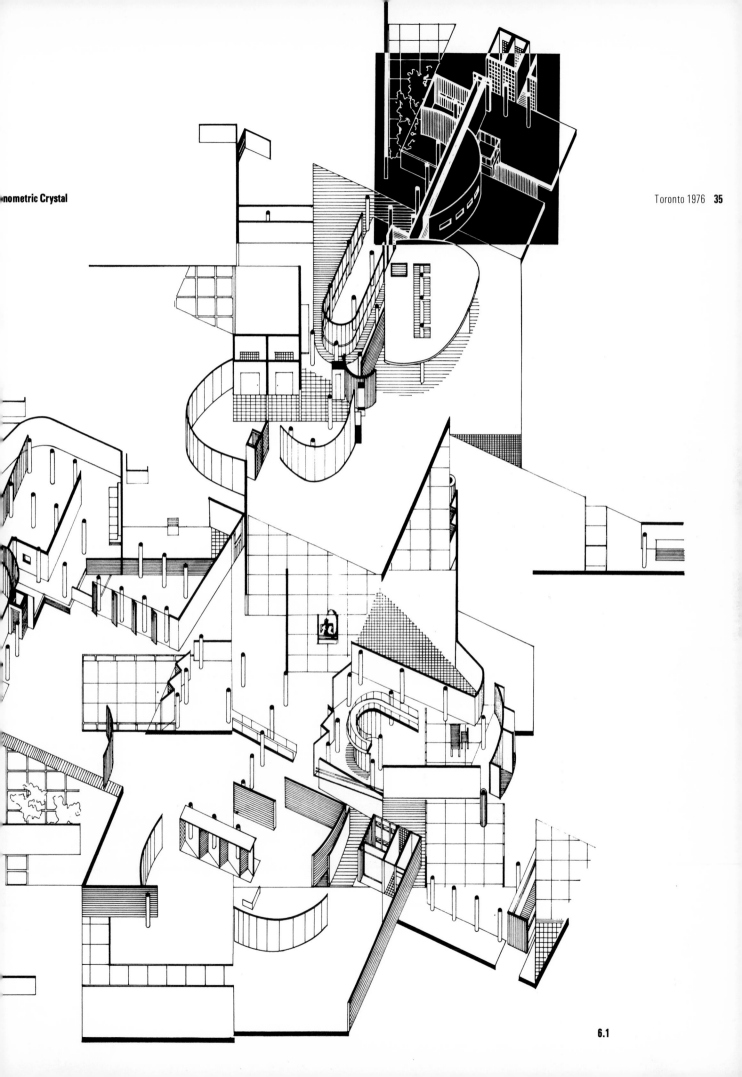

6.1

6

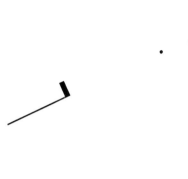

6.2

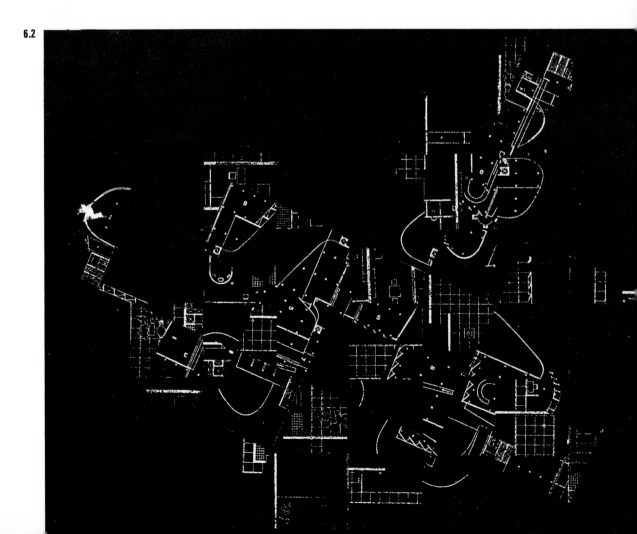

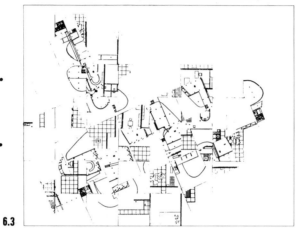

6.3

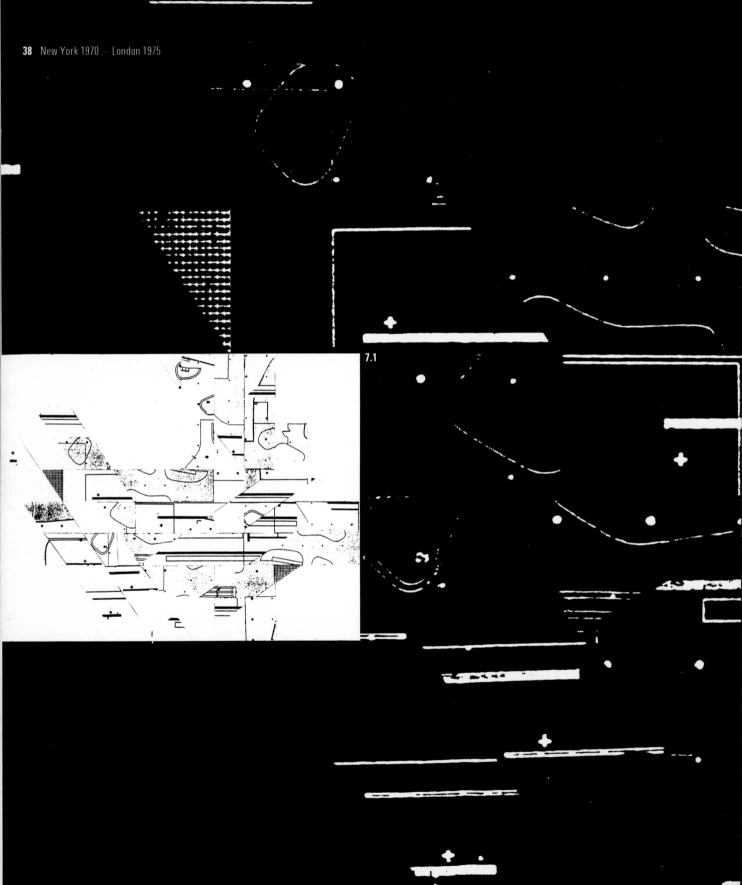

7.1

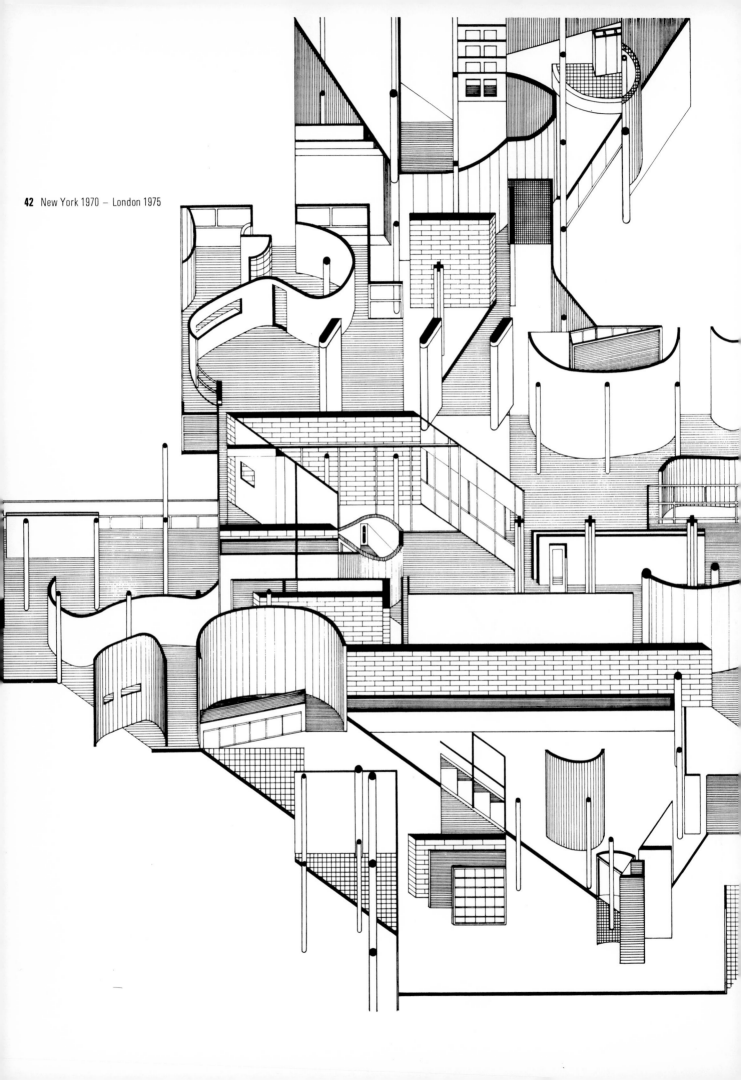

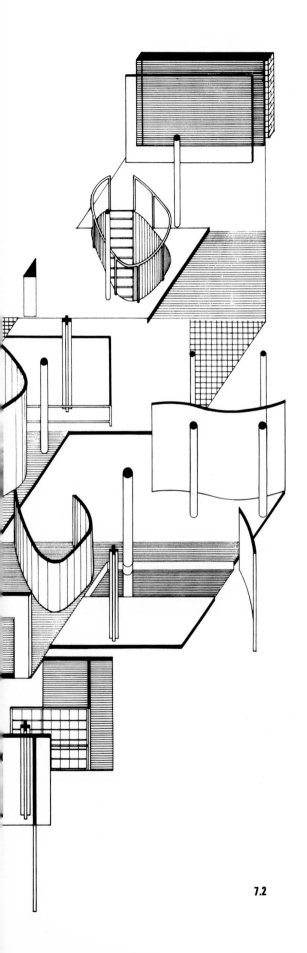

7.2

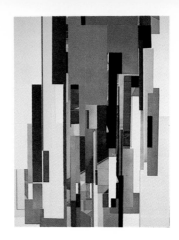

7 Collage Rebus 2 model

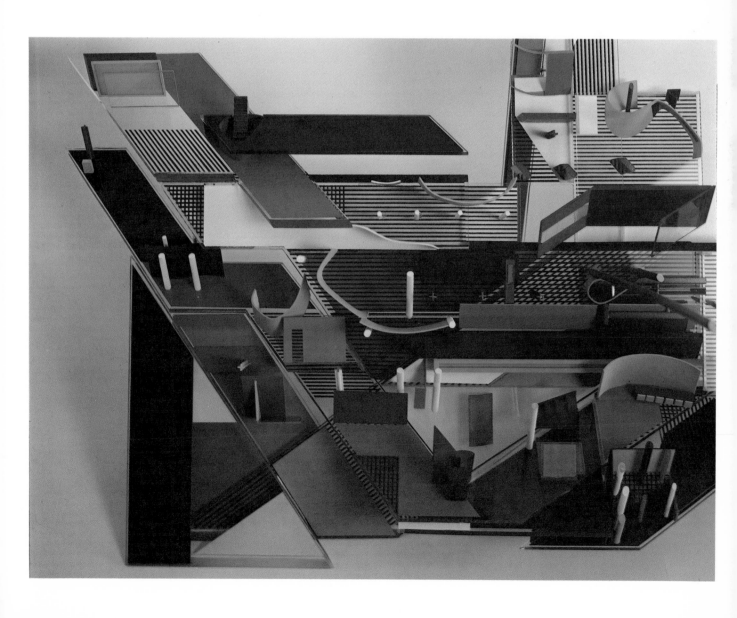

46 New York 1970 – London 1975

Collage Rebus 2 model

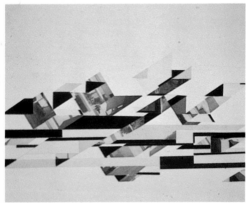

8.2 Axonometric Crystal

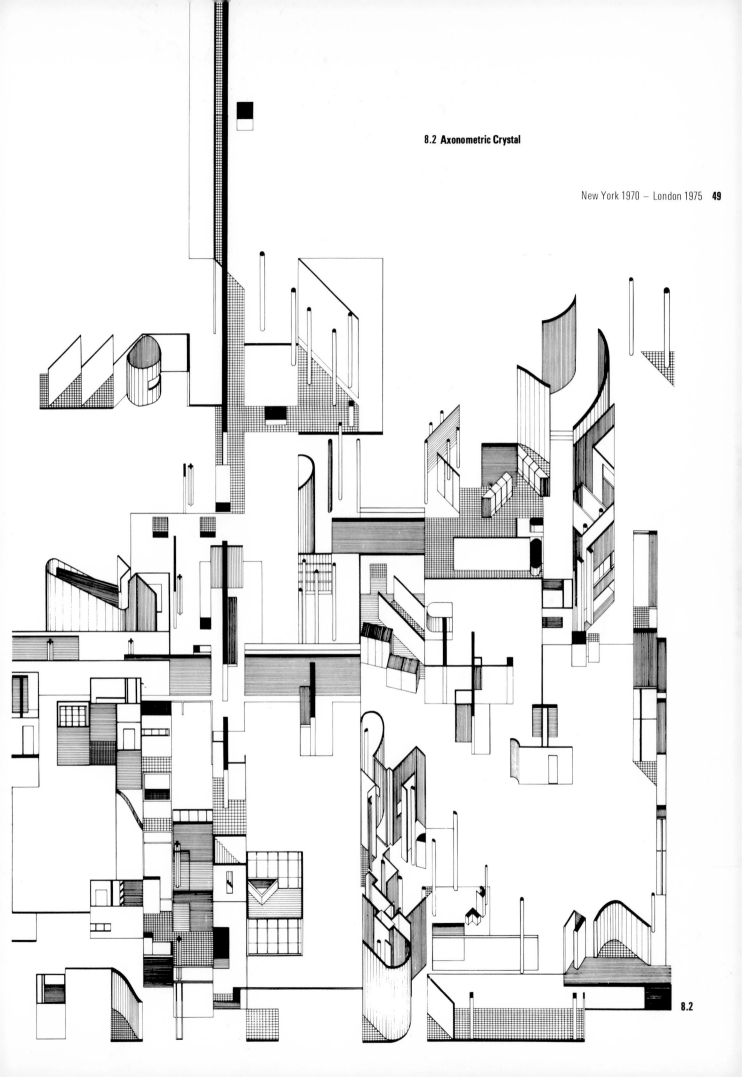

8.2

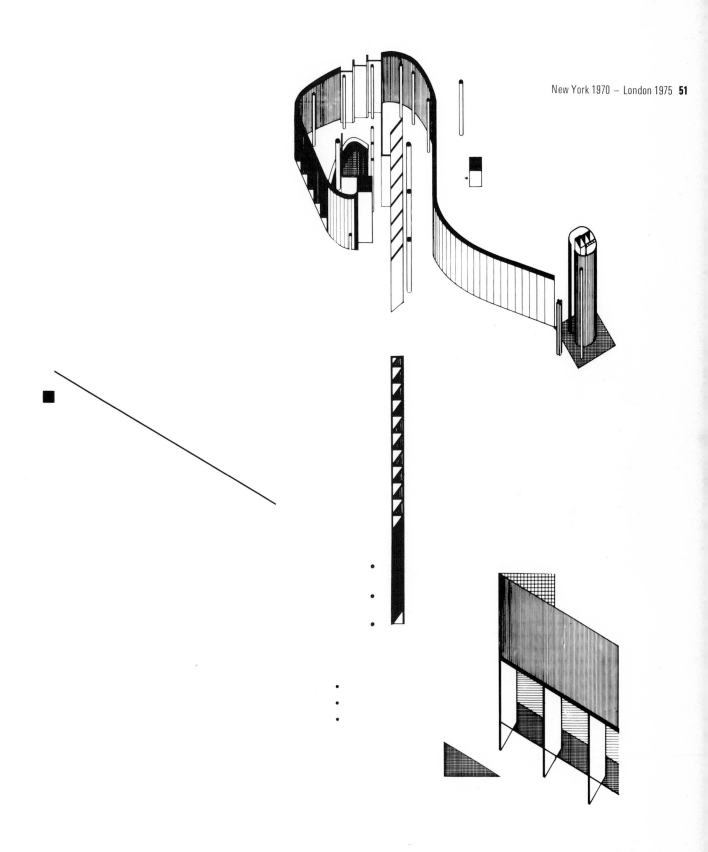

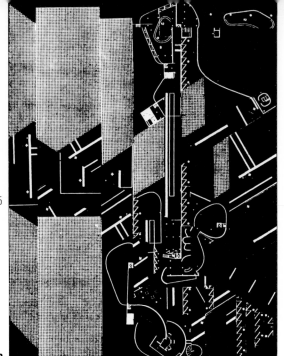

52 New York 1970 – London 1975

9.2

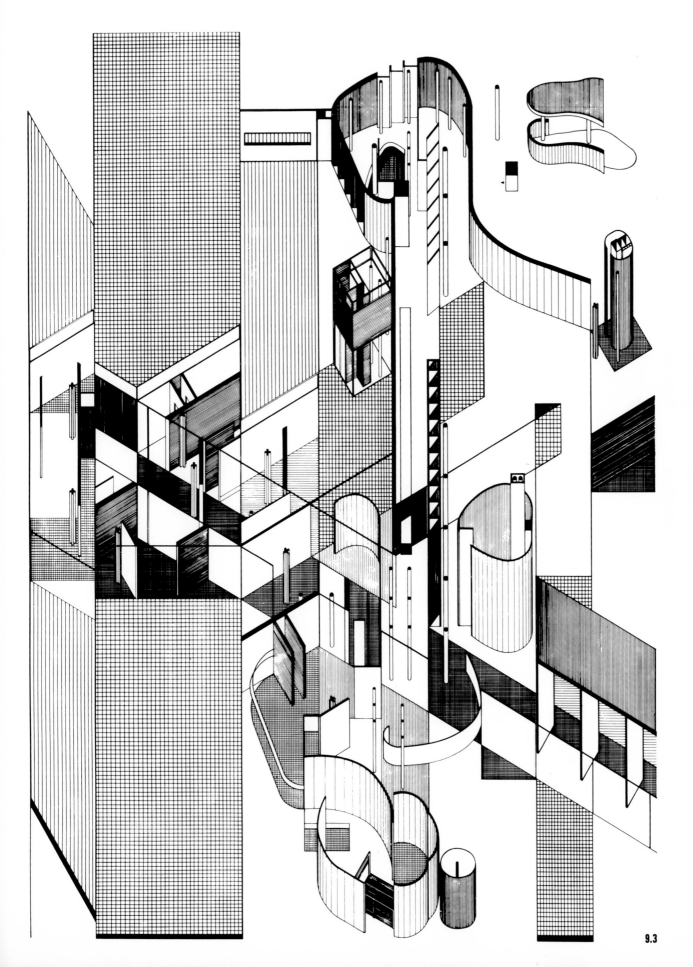

9.2 Schema

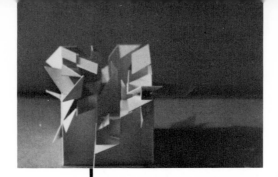

10 EXEMPLARY REDUCTION OF A 'HOUSE WITH A FRONT LAWN', UNDER THE SIGN OF TIME.

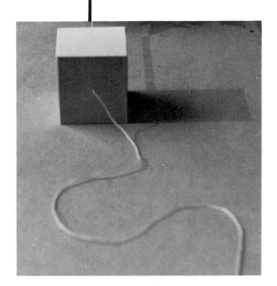

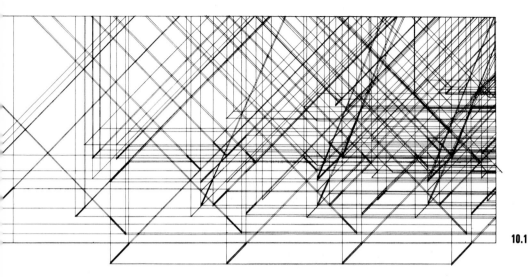

10.1

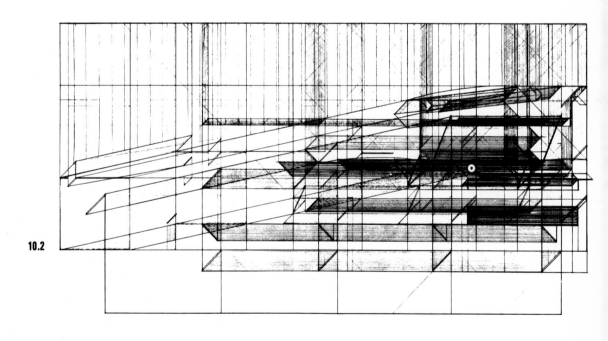

10.2

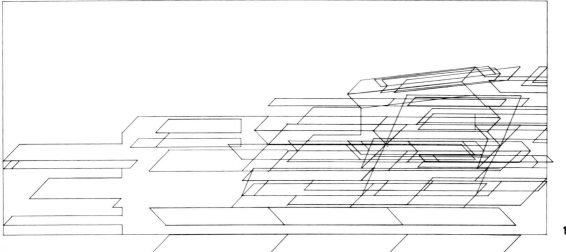

10.3

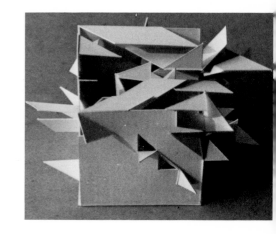

10

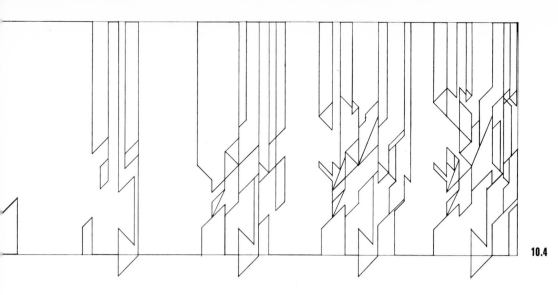

10.4

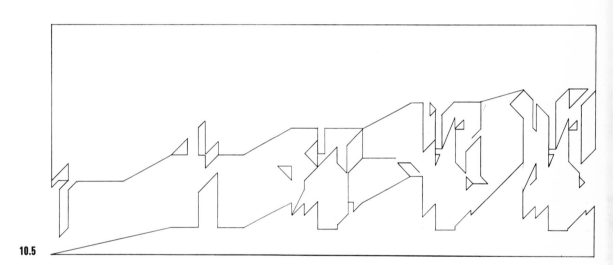

10.5

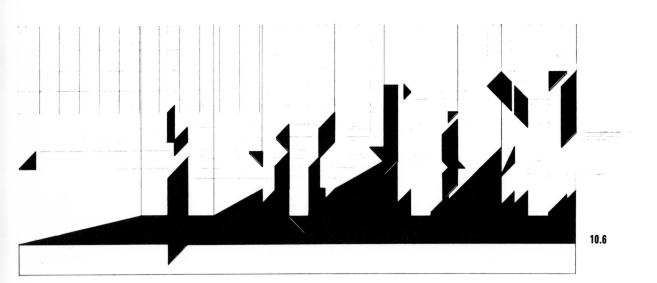

10.6

10

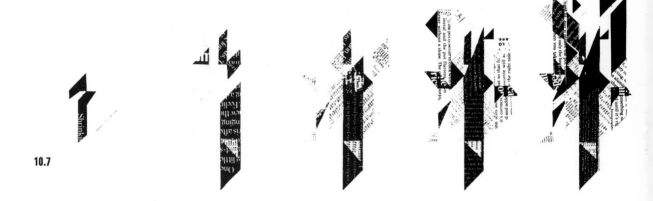

10.7

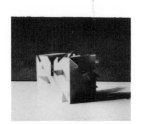

10

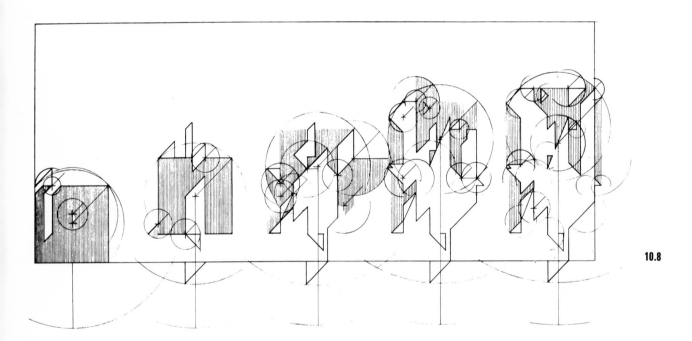

10.8

10.9

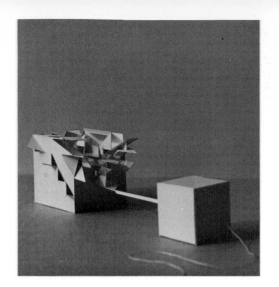

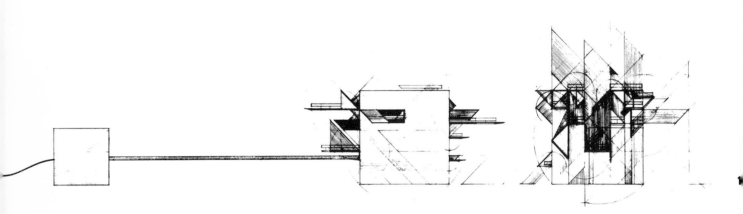

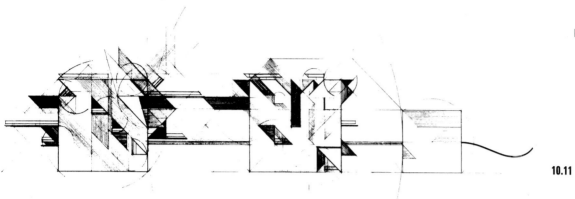

10.11

10

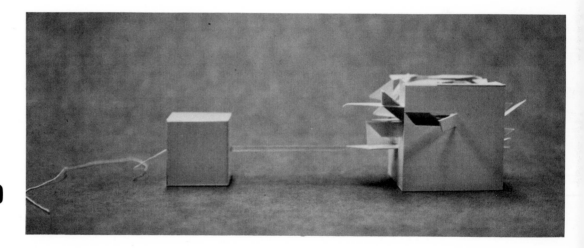

10

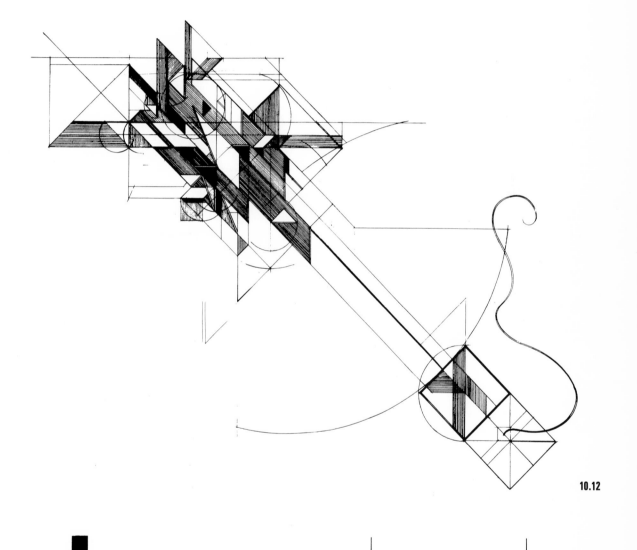

10.12

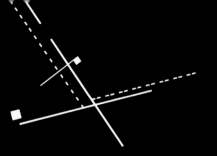

11 THE OTHER SIDE: IKON AND IDEA

11.1

11.1 "The Seduction of the Future" collage

11.2 "Janus" (Cosmetics of Fear) collage

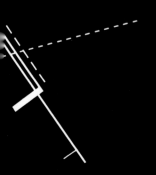

11.3 "Berenice and Ligeia" collage

11.4 "England" collage

11.4

11

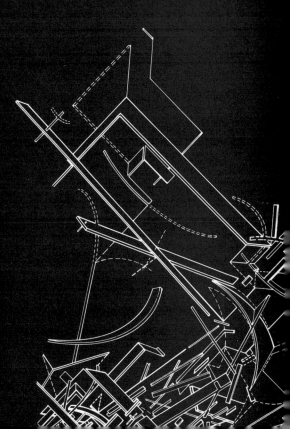

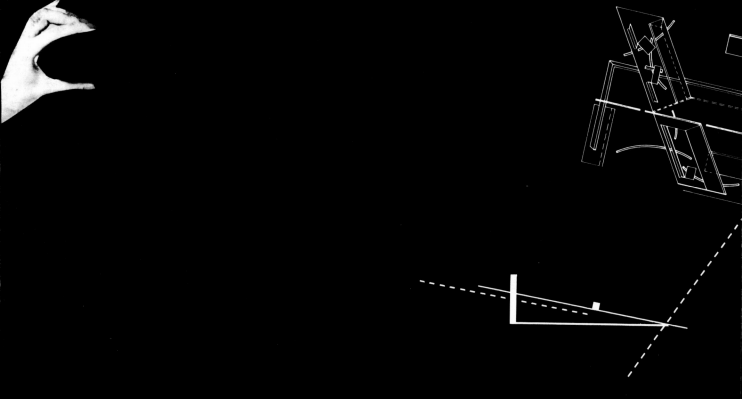

11.8   11.9

11

11.10

'It is the necessary destiny of culture that everything which it creates in its constituent process removes us more and more from the originality of life. The more richly and energetically the human spirit engages its formative activity the further this very activity seems to remove it from the primal source of its own being. More and more, it appears to be imprisoned in its own creations, which cover it like a delicate and transparent but unbreakable veil... If all Culture is manifested in the creation of a specific image-world, of specific symbolic forms, the aim of understanding is not to go beyond all these creations, but rather to understand and elucidate their basic formative principle. It is solely through the awareness of this principle that the content of life acquires its true form.'

E. Cassirer

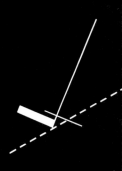

11.5

11.6

11.7

11

''The most beautiful order of the world
is still a random gathering of things
insignificant in themselves.''

Heraclitus

11.13

11

11.14

11.11

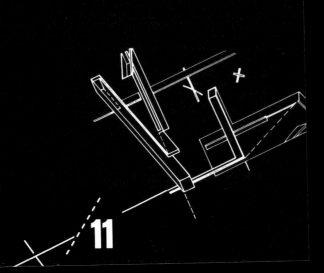

11

11.12

11.15 "Why? Who? What?" collage

"About the four hundred and fiftieth year of his age, or latter end of his childhood, he dissected a great number of small insects not more than one hundred feet in diameter, which are not perceivable by ordinary microscopes, of which he composed a very curious treatise, which involved him in some trouble."

VOLTAIRE

MICROMEGAS

micromegas
THE ARCHITECTURE OF END SPACE

N°:

THIS IS OF A LIMITED EDITION OF **30** NUMBERED AND SIGNED PORTFOLIOS

D. LIBESKIND

END SPACE

Daniel Libeskind
Cranbrook

80

Architectural drawings have in modern times assumed the identity of signs; they have become the fixed and silent accomplices in the overwhelming endeavour of building and construction. In this way, their own open and unknowable horizon has been reduced to a level which proclaims the **a priori** coherence of technique. In considering them as mere technical adjuncts, collaborating in the execution of a series made up of self-evident steps, they have appeared as either self-effacing materials or as pure formulations cut off from every external reference.

While the classical axiomatic of architectural drawing elaborated its usefulness within an overall theory of order, by beginning with well-established theories of representation and attempting to unify them, contemporary formal systems present themselves as riddles - unknown instruments for which usage is yet to be found. Today, we seldom start with particular conditions which we raise to a general view; rather we descend from a general system to a particular problem. However, what is significant in this tendency (where the relation between the abstract and the concrete is reversed) is the claim which disengages the nature of drawing, as though the 'reduction' of drawing were an amplification of the mechanisms of knowledge; an instrument capable of revealing, at a stroke, new areas of the 'real'.

There is a historical tradition in architecture, whereby drawings (as well as other forms of communication) signify more than can be embodied in stabilized frameworks of objectifiable data. If we can go beyond the material carrier (sign) into the internal reality of a drawing, the reduction of representation to a formal system - seeming at first void and useless - begins to appear as an extension of reality which is quite natural. The system ceases to be perceived as a prop whose coherence is supported by empty symbols, and reveals a structure whose manifestation is only mediated by symbolism.

An architectural drawing is as much a prospective unfolding of future possibilities as it is a recovery of a particular history to whose intentions it testifies and whose limits it always challenges. In any case a drawing is more than the shadow of an object, more than a pile of lines, more than a resignation to the inertia of convention.

The act of creation in the order of procedures of imagination, h elsewhere, coincides with creation in the objective realm. Dra not mere invention; its efficacy is not drawn from its own unli resources of liberty. It is a state of experience in which the 'o revealed through mechanisms which provoke and support obj accomplishments as well as supporting the one who draws up them. Being neither pure registration nor pure creation, thes ings come to resemble an explication or a reading of a pre-giv a text both generous and inexhaustible.

I am interested in the profound relation which exists between tuition of geometric structure as it manifests itself in a pre-ob sphere of experience and the possibility of formalization which to overtake it in the objective realm. In fact, these seemingly sive attitudes polarize the movement of imagination and give impression of discontinuity, when in reality they are but differ reciprocal moments - alternative viewpoints - of the same fun tal, ontological necessity.

We cannot simply oppose the formal to the non-formal withou same time destroying the mobility, variation and effectiveness nated in the very nature of formalism. From a certain point of everything is formalism; the distinction between 'perspective 'figure' (depth and flatness) - which seems definitive - branch and distributes itself over layers of intentionality which in rea show a continuity more than a difference. In a parallel analog seems to be supported by the empirical significance of signs t selves, which magnify appearances by reducing structure to t

My work attempts to express this inadequacy at the heart of p tion for which no (final) terms are provided; a lack of fulfillme prevents manifestation being reducible to an object-datum. O horizons, in relation to time, can forms appear in this explorat the 'marginal' where concepts and premonitions overlap. The presentation, but always according to the mode of imperfectio internal play in which deferred completeness is united with a r ized openness. The work remains an indefinite series because dialectic cannot be halted. As such, these drawings and collag develop in an area of architectural thinking which is neither a nor a poetics of space.

Because the 'geometry of experience' is only a horizon of potential formalization and we find it already inserted into that other horizon of desire and intuition, the task of essential clarification, as I see it, becomes the systematic and dynamic transmutation of movements; an exchange between abstract cyphers, exhausted in their own objectivity and hardened in fixed signs, and concrete contingencies responsive to the permanent solicitations of a spontaneous appeal.

An authentic abstraction gives us what is most unique in incomplete but formalized levels of grasping objects. It does so because at first uniqueness is given in an impure fashion, blended as it is with elements representing categories of experience which must be progressively extracted from the general alienation of over-qualified intuition of spatial structure. This 'purification' attempts, through a series of successive steps, to realize the elimination of intuitive content and numerical relations, and leads to ever more encompassing (spherical) possibilities of configuration.

But through an enigmatic reversal, one discovers in this ascent (or escape?) through the 'funnel' of an increasingly precise effort of projection, a regression toward the unique and primordial condition of metrics. The vectorial 'going beyond' is, at the same time, a deepening spiral movement which exposes this transgression as a moment of a concentric approach. In this sense, an overall envelopment neutralizes tension and reveals a foundation both of continuity and change: a homogeneous state pervades even the most complex antinomies.

Most of all, however, I am a fascinated observer and a perplexed participant of that mysterious desire which seeks a radical elucidation of the original precomprehension of forms - an ambition which I think is implicit in all architecture. If there is true abstraction here (as opposed to generalization) it is not achieved by the elimination of contents through a gradual deployment of an increasing emptiness, but is rather an isolation of structural essence, whose manifestation in two dimensions illuminates all the sub-systems of projection (for example, three-dimensional space).

Edmund Husserl's **The Origin Of Geometry** has been an inspiration to me in all these 'researches'. Understanding that the historical genesis of geometry evolved from the problems of land-surveying (as calculus originated from the study of movement, or statistics from the study of collectivities) I have become increasingly aware of the fact that the disclosure of the first horizon (outlining the space of initial encounters) also guarantees the 'leakage' in the project of objectification. The same structures which we have already experienced in a confused and pre-reflective situation are continually transposed to a reflective realm where they open the way for ever more elaborated descriptions. It is not a matter of piling superimposed hierarchies one on top of another, rather the trajectory of intentions transposes content into operation and at the same time displaces descriptive geometry by the structural. The transformation of object into operation imposes a temporal dimension on this process; a process whose meaning is not arbitrary and yet is not predetermined either.

The invisible ground from which it is possible to scaffold moving layers of construction enables one to recover modes of awareness quite removed from the initial hypothesis of rationality. These drawings seek to reflect, on a deeper level of consciousness, the inner life of geometrical order whose nucleus is the conflict between the Voluntary and the Involuntary. Once again this duality (like that of realism-formalism) appears as an unsurpassable condition pointing to a dynamic ground which testifies to an experience which receives only as much as it is capable of giving; draws only that which allows itself to be drawn into.

12 MICROMEGAS

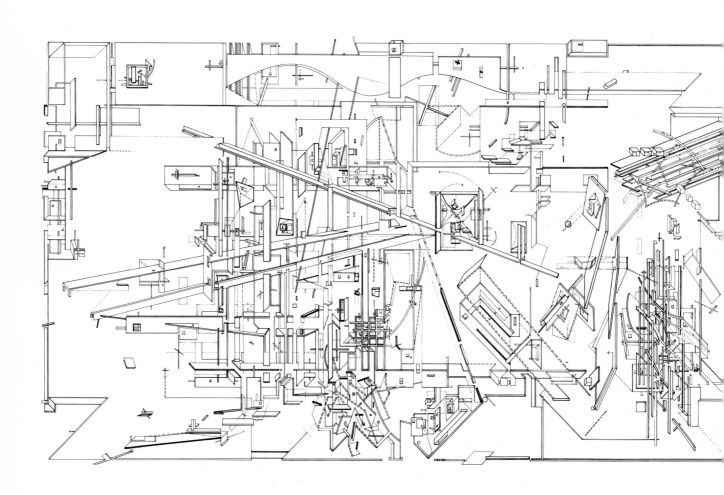

12.1

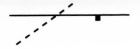

12.2 Time Sections

12.1 The Garden

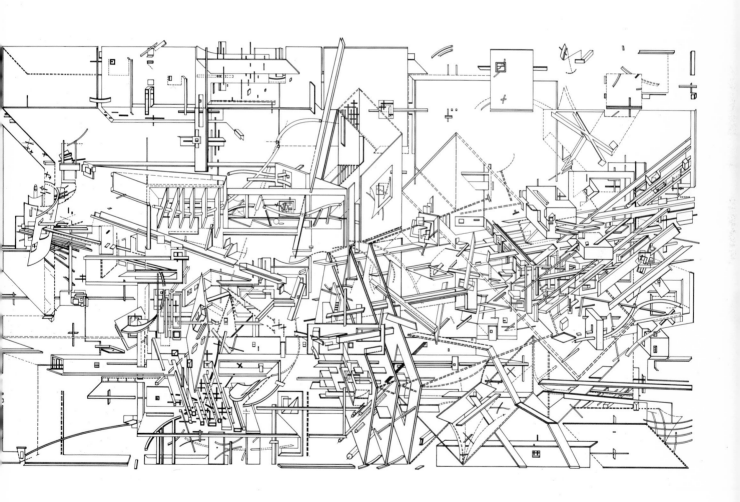

12.2

84 Cranbrook 1979

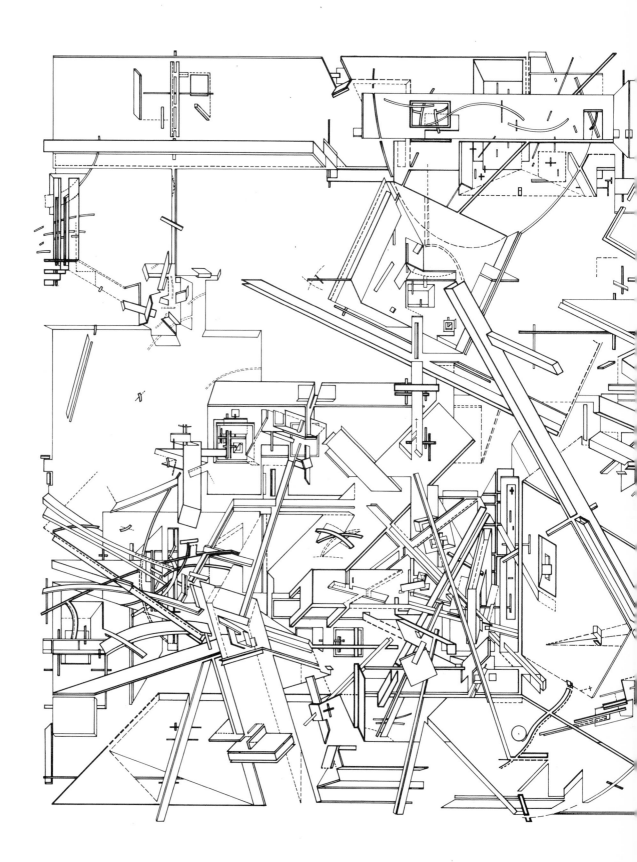

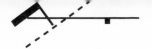

12.3 Leakage

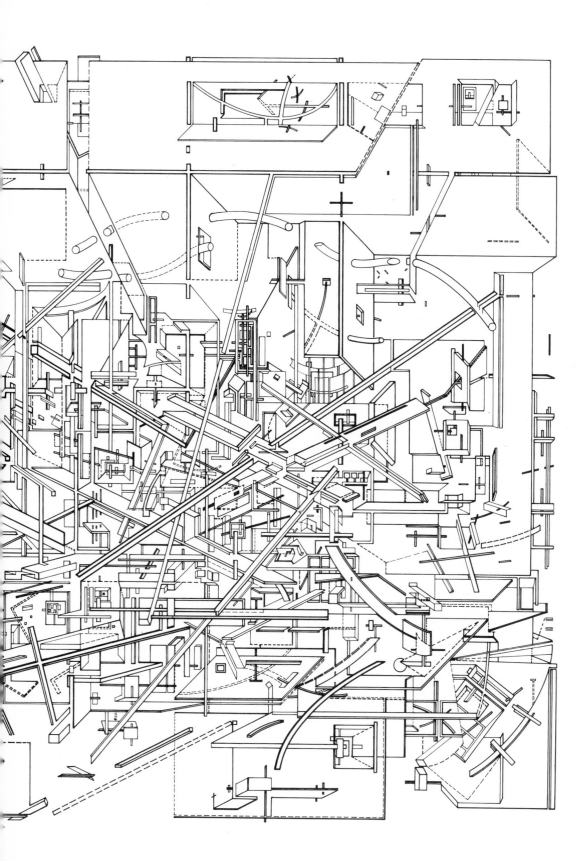

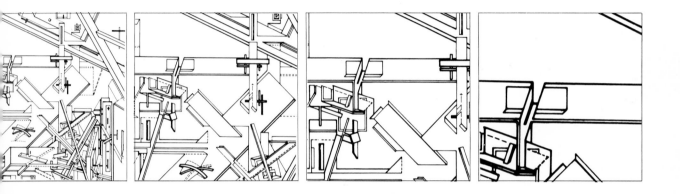

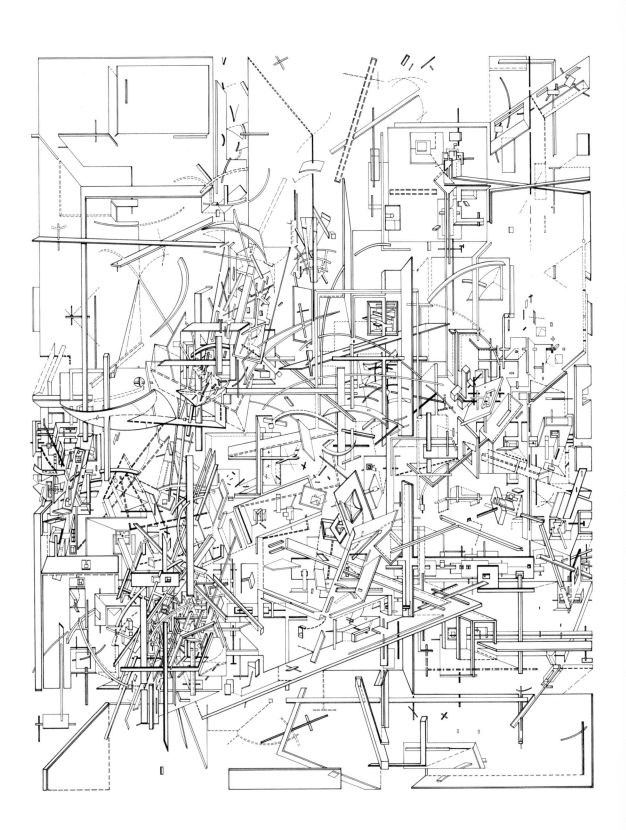

12.4

12.5 Micromegas #3: Leakage, (wood model, fragment)

12.4 Little Universe

12.5

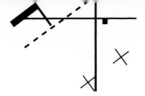

90 Cranbrook 1979

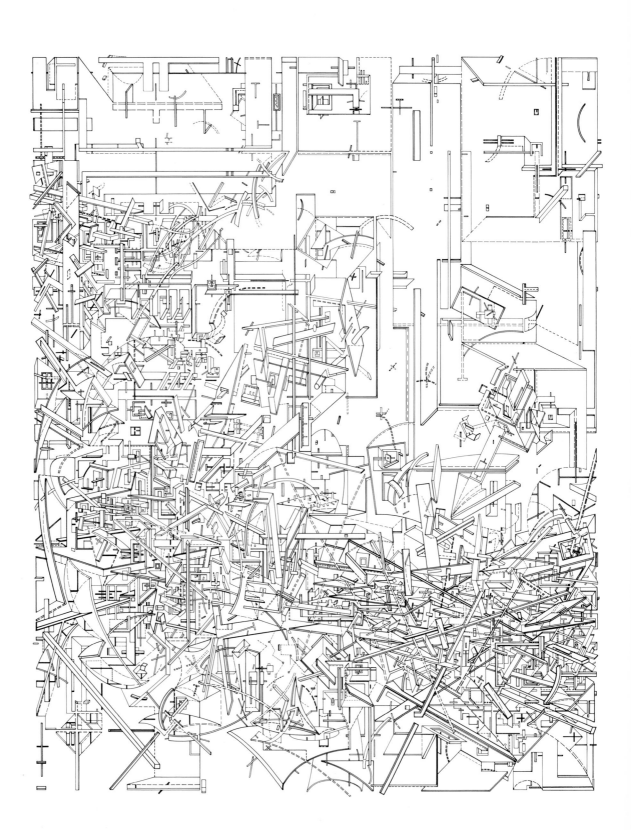

12.6

12.7 Micromegas #3: Leakage, (metal model, fragment)

12.6 Arctic Flowers

12.7

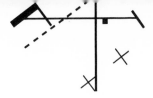

92 Cranbrook 1979

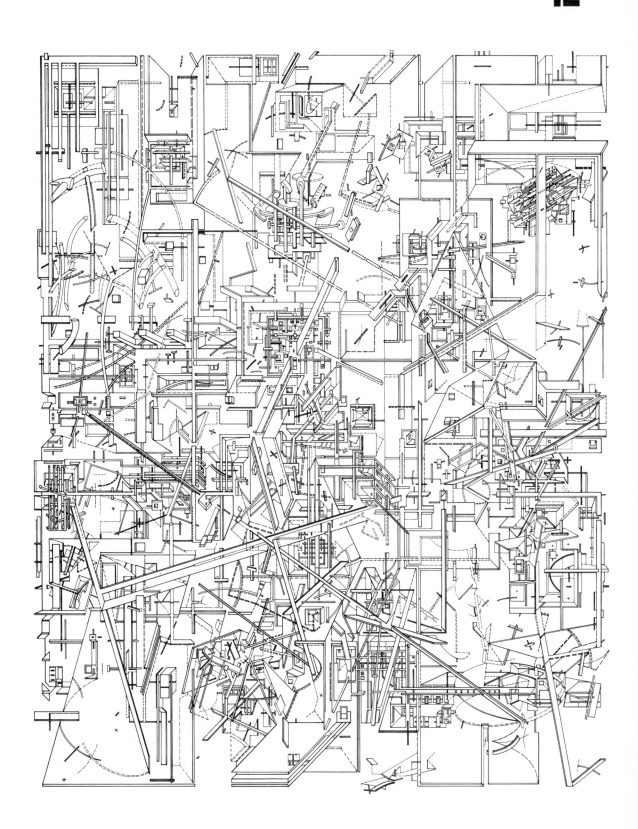

12.8

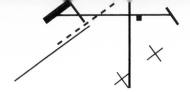

12.8 The Burrow Laws   **12.9 Maldoror's Equation**

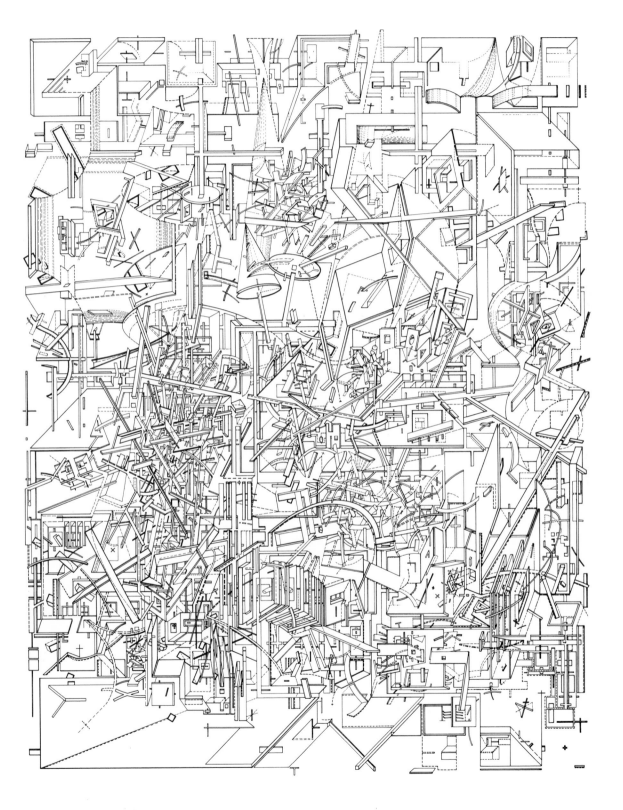

12.9

94 Cranbrook 1979

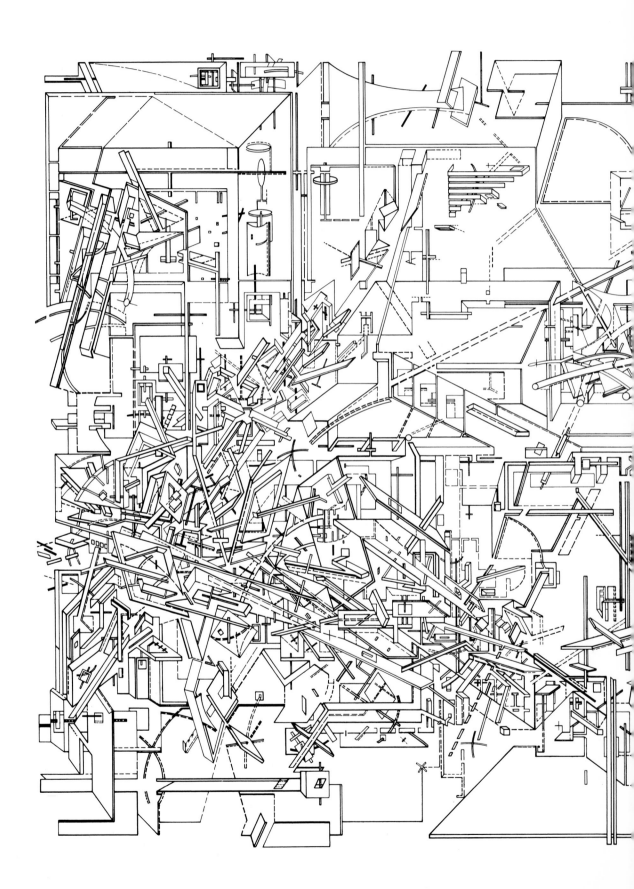

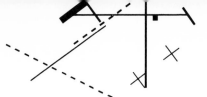

12.10   Dance Sounds

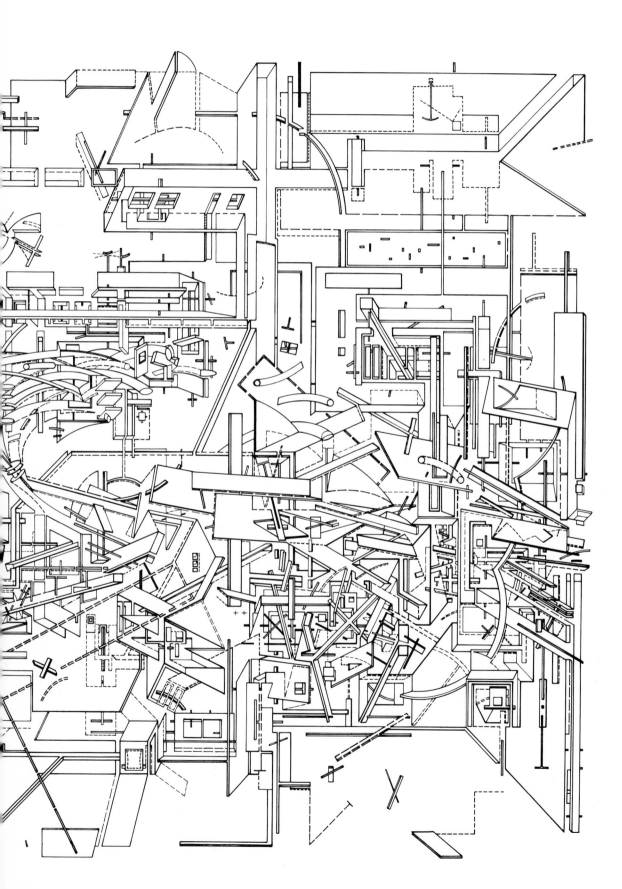

details

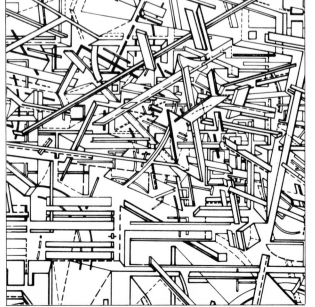

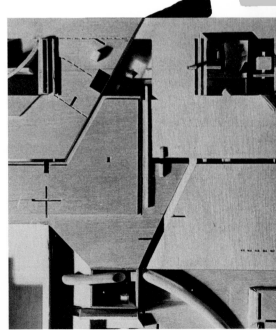

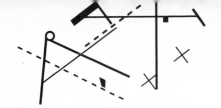

12.11

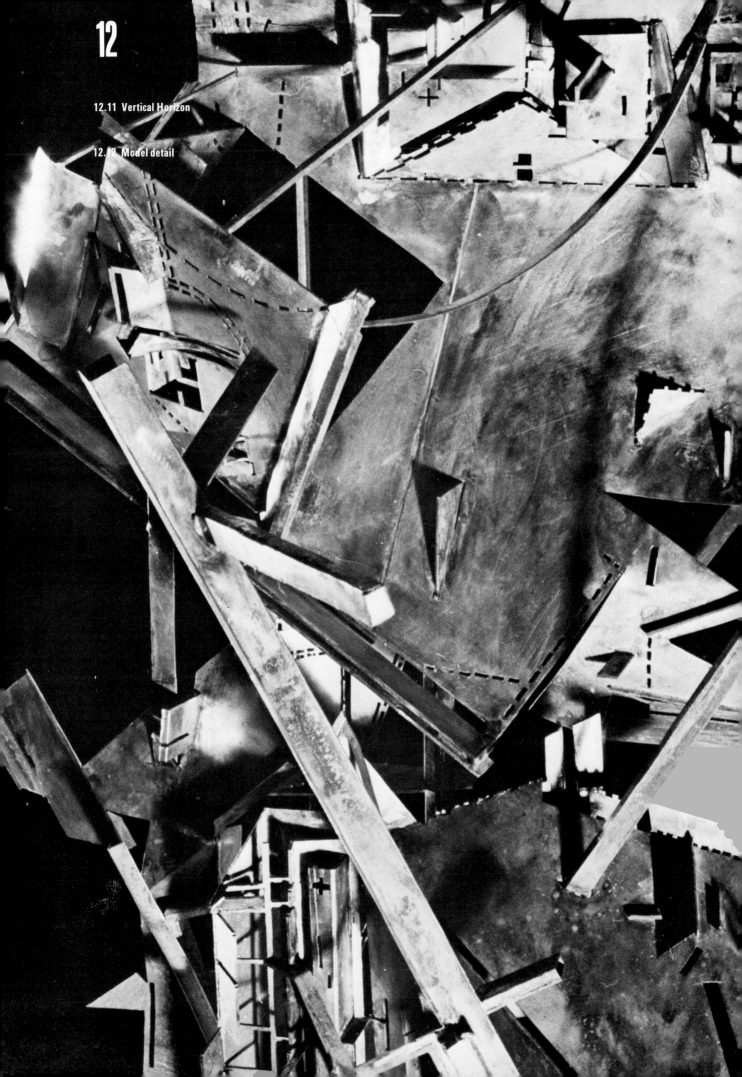

12

12.11 Vertical Horizon

12.12 Model detail

12

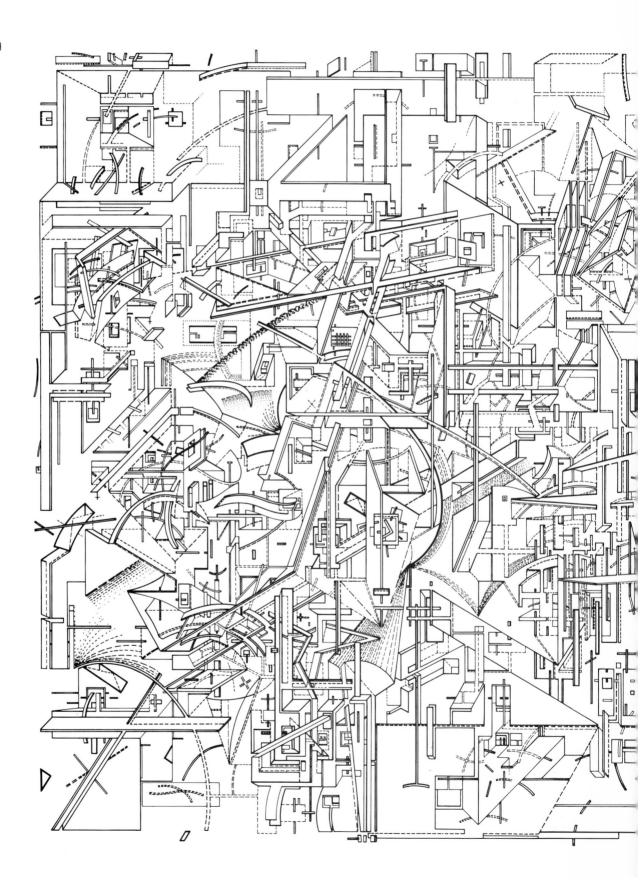

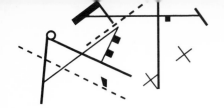

12.13 Dream Calculus

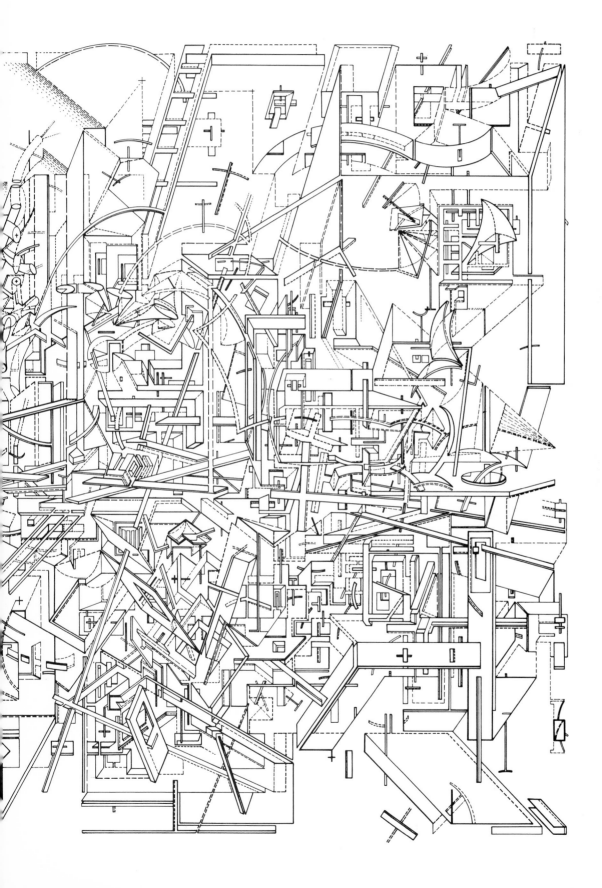

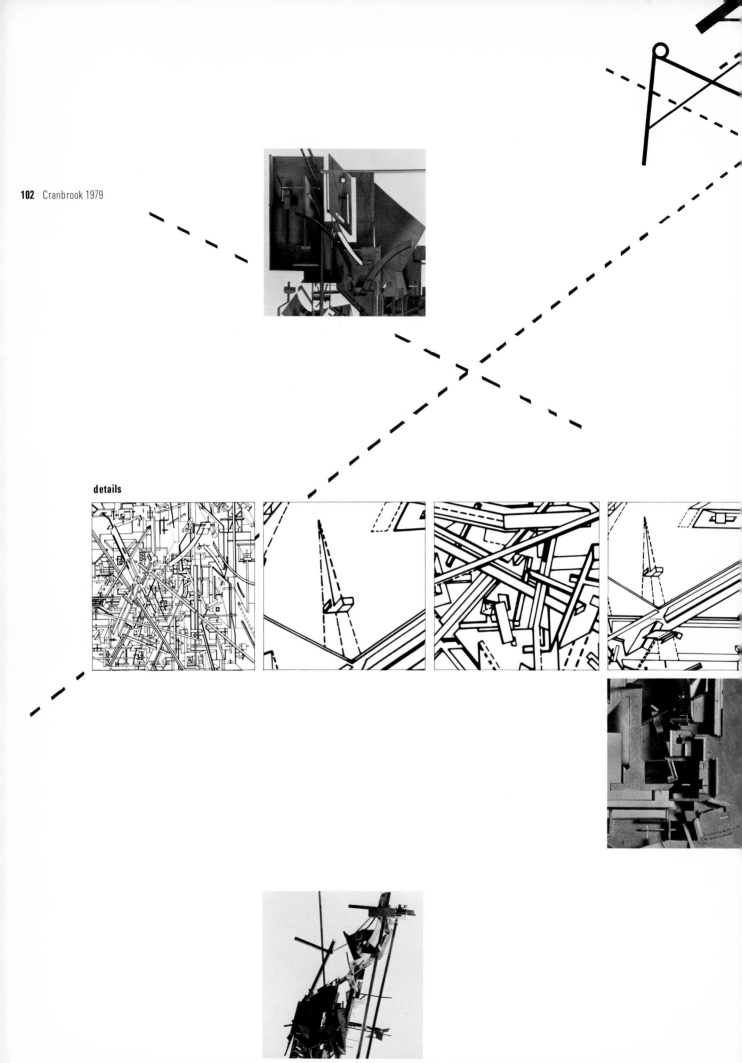

details

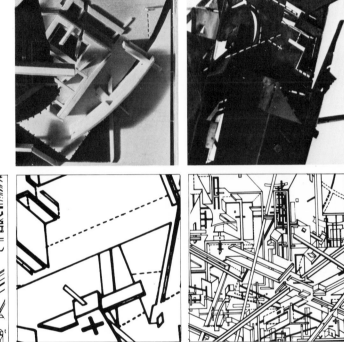

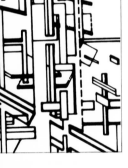

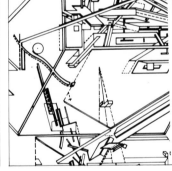

IMAGES IN THE LIBESKIND MACROSCOPE

John Hejduk
New York

Juhani Pallasmaa
Director, Museum of
Finnish Architecture

104

There is an explosion... into space... soundless. The debris is float-
ing in a universe devoid of an ending; but with a difference. Each
particle; each element; each sign; each figure; each shape; each plan;
each thought is still intact... precise.

Although on a two-dimensional sheet of paper, the implied vacuum is
understood to be a spherical ground; a semi-sphere. As in film, the
space is three-quarter depth.

There is no exit; no escape; from the time... the time it takes to pene-
trate. Our minds are shattered by the involvement. There is no pro-
tection for our eyes... we are simply drawn into... to a mysterious; a
phenomenological; ...a profound new vision.

The conflagration of interweaving; of intertwined; of interconnected
notes are... film stopped... stopped into a frame of silent time... a
state of the exact present of no time... At first we sense that our
brain; our eyes; are compressed accordion-like into the surface...
telescoping takes place. The front of our iris is in immediate contact
with the physicality of an idea. We are afraid that our retina may be
damaged...we are in danger...there is a tendency to leave this apoc-
ryphal determinate alone...best not to cross over...yet we have
been netted. Shards of memory lie everywhere... exposed... dare we
pick them up? Those fragments can cut deep... they have an interna-
lity. Perhaps they be the acupunctures to the soul? How is it that rev-
volutions take on such a religious zeal? The drawings speak of hospi-
tals too... drainage tubes are everywhere. Are they helping to keep
abstraction alive? Was abstraction wounded by blunt propositions?
Is it a projection of how the after battle-field of the bio-sphere could
look? Are we looking at the first X-ray of the 'city of the mind'? Yes,
our mind-soul must look like that... moments of density moving to-
wards a vanishing point. The periphery recorded in empty gaps. It is
worrisome... traps everywhere... to fall into perpetual float. This
could be a place where a modern Virgil might accompany a new
Dante. They go as voyeurs into the bone field of abandoned constructivism... blown alive to haunt the cerebellum. Pyramid tops prick
toes... cries of pinioned mathematics!!!

The first musical score of a new age? Of the old age? The density of a
Proust page without words? The dance of cacophonic geometries?
Torques of no redemption? A dissection is taking place. The scatter-
ing of species. There can be no trees in this garden... all chlorophyll
has been extracted... a celebration of essences. The umbilical cord of
architecture is shown. Dare it be cut?

Danny Libeskind is an authentic original. Our hearts are with the
architectural histories of the past when our eyes comprehend architectural realities of the present. Old building elements are always in
the present. It is our minds that speculate on architectural futures;
knowing full well it is all a helix spiralling in space, moving from a
darkness to a darkness.

We are witness to the occurrence of an architectural birth.

∎

When I saw Daniel's drawings, executed with meticulous per
I knew immediately that these architectonic visions interprete
multi-dimensional space-time experience. The complex inter
of several simultaneous projections, constant shifting of scale
ence, and the endlessness of space launched an instant train
associations

... secret scores for astronomical rites...
... El Lissitsky's Prouns to second power...
... encyclopaedia of architectural motives...
... sound clusters of Ligeti and Panderetski in visual form...

Instead of being balanced, finite compositions of volumes in v
experienced the images as architectural narratives without be
or end, and as passionate explorations in tectonic space, remi
of Piranesi's forceful **Carceri d'Invenzione** visions. The exper
space was not, however, literal or illusory - the eye was not los
depths, but was returned safely to the surface. I felt Daniel's
thorough knowledge of philosophy and history merge into his
talent.

Before even learning the title of his **Micromega** series - dedica
the Great Satirist - I had the paradoxical scale associations of a
architectural Milky Way or an explosion of the Tectonic Nucle
Were these images architectural metaphors of the initial or th
inal explosion?

A feeling of an intentional satire on the history of the Modern
ment also entered my mind - the lines of Voltaire that Daniel h
chosen as the motto for his series are a shameless mockery on
reader's perceptual limits. Associations of music and the aud
the forms and their configurations and collisions were equally
Here I felt the presence of the musician in Daniel's personalit

I was so moved by the images of his macroscope that next nig
hotel room I had a strangely metaphysical dream. The dream
to be a direct deep-structure echo of my preceding experience

A group of us had learned the secret - at a certain moment of t
the bells of Alvar Aalto's Assisian hillside church at Muurame
made to ring by a ray of the falling sun. We are waiting in the
ening temple, in suspense, as the ray approaches its target. T
great disappointment the gloomy silence continues on past th
moment the ray has finally struck the bronze surface. Our gro
embarrassment and frustration are suddenly interrupted by a
tolling of the bell. The violent sound keeps thundering around
valley, arousing the anger of the villagers.

We are utterly perplexed at the unexpected course of events u
dawns on us that the sun was not to make the bell toll, but our
thought.

∎

THE DRAMA OF THE ENDGAME

Dalibor Veseley
London

The visual reality of Daniel Libeskind's drawings is situated very far beyond the reality of cubism, constructivism or collage, close to the horizon where most of the non-figurative movements of this century fought their last battles and where our imagination is permanently challenged by the inner possibilities of abstraction. It is obviously possible to be calm and resist the challenge by poetic analysis and interpretation of the drawings as they appear and end up with a description of imaginary landscapes, cities etc. which they seemingly represent. It is also possible, however, to accept the challenge and be drawn into a very different world - the world of ambiguous visual metaphors and fragments of objects in a dramatic process of trans-formations and projections - or, to use the author's own words, 'deconstructive constructions'. At this point there is no doubt that the main intention behind the drawings is to explore the limits of the representative power of our imagination vis-a-vis the conceptual possibilities which exist in current architecture and the visual arts and not to create an elaborate and careful construction in a universe parallel to our own.

It is not surprising that the method used most consistently in the drawings is one of projective geometries, which has a very long and well-established tradition, going back to the artists of Italian manner-ism and their art of anamorphosis, and which has also been so far a most successful method for following visually the inner possibilities of thought far into imaginary reality.

The poetic qualities of such exploration have been recognized and fully appreciated by the surrealists. 'One cannot fail to be struck by the fact that it was in 1870, the year when both Lautreamont and Rimbaud began separately to emit the shock waves of sensibility which increased steadily in power and still affect us deeply at the present time, that mathematicians elaborated a generalized geom-etry which included Euclidean geometry as part of a comprehen-sive system and so redeemed it from its temporary eclipse. This involved the same kind of transcended contradiction which Lautreamont and Rimbaud used in a different field.' (A. Breton)

In either case we are witnessing the same stirrings of the thought re-belling against established habits of thinking and heralding a way of thought which has become infinitely more inductive and extensible, and which has produced a crisis that modern art has identified as the 'crisis of an object'. 'The object ceases to be fixed permanently on the near side of thought and recreates itself on the further side as far as the eye can reach.' (A. Breton) With this new focus, the same object, however complete it may seem, reverts to an infinite series of latent possibilities which are not peculiar to it and therefore entail its transformation. The object's conventional meaning then becomes en-tirely subordinate to its transformational meaning.

The analogy with contemporary literature may help us to understand better what is taking place in the drawings. Much of this century, literature has been written in a paradigmatic form. Unlike a linear form, which is essentially purposive and with a sense of direction, the paradigmatic form is circular; the same movement of thought is very often repeated, re-covering similar ground but rendering the move-ment richer and fuller with every passing. This makes us see in the end the text as constant transformation, as possible meaning the transformations may bring. The drawings reveal a very similar

form. Traditional geometry with muted historical references - Durer, P. della Francesca etc. - is gradually transformed into less intuitive forms in a repeated movement of projections (very similar to the eidetic variation in Husserlian phenomenology) creating a sequence of geometrical nodes that form and dissolve before us. Not only do such projections create new meanings, they create new con-texts in which meaning may occur. The result is a bizarre interplay of forms, which can be identified, and meaning, which can only be anti-cipated.

In his novel **Dans le Labyrinth** Robbe-Grillett begins with a descrip-tion of a room. Outside is a soldier standing under a street lamp. The author describes the room carefully, devoting great attention to a pic-ture hanging on the wall. The picture represents a cafe scene which suddenly comes to life. The door in the cafe opens and the same sol-dier walks in. The novel transforms one plane of reality into the next, until the only reality that one can trust is the reality of the printed word, it is an integral part of the word itself and of its particular sit-uation.

The analogy between the text and the drawings is at this point almost complete. The only difference that remains is the more concrete real-ity of the word, which may help us to see better the meaning of the visual and more abstract reality of the drawings. This is particularly relevant in the case of those drawings which have been directly in-spired by literary text, such as 'Maldoror's equation' for instance. The analogy with Lautreamont's imagery of precision, sharp geom-etric forms, cutting, verticality and flight reveal an even more impor-tant analogy with the deep and truly epochal meaning of the text - the attempt to overcome the confines of culture and to transcend the limitations of the human condition.

The major instrument of transcendence has always been mathematics because it generates its own development regardless of whether or not what is developed can be reconciled with the rest of the reality. The geometrical density of Daniel Libeskind's drawings illustrates how tortuous and irrational such a reconciliation could be, and how close is the dream of transcendence to the enigma of the labyrinth. The labyrinth is not in this case the work of a calculating craftsman but the result of a drama in which the calculating imagination has been con-fronted with its own unexpected products, too ambiguous and in the end impenetrable.

■

"The green membranes of space..."

Lautreamont

"Is the no-longer-metaphysical already
included in the not-yet-metaphysical?"

Heidegger

Cranbrook 1980 **107**

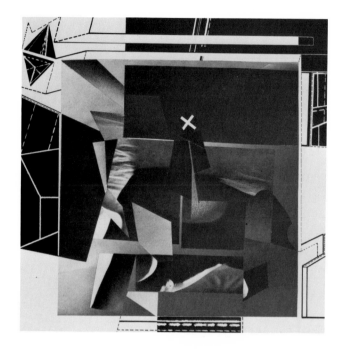

VAIN AMUSEMENTS

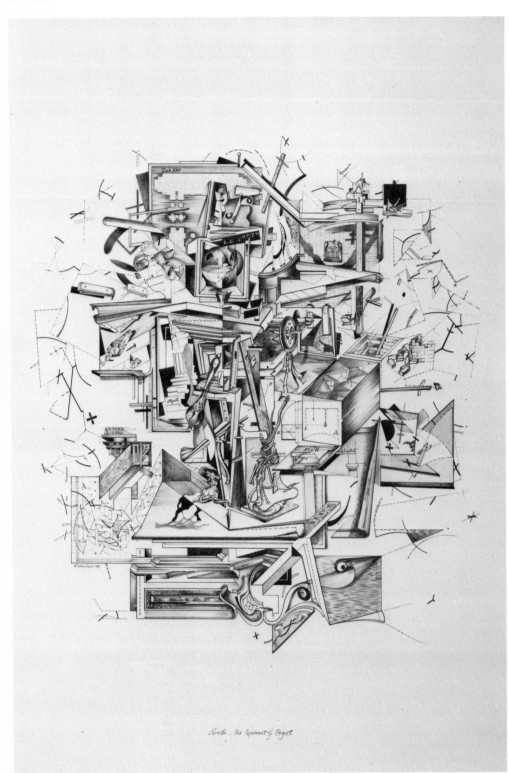

14.2

The History of Vegetables and so forth

14.3

THE GRIM REAPER

14.4

OSSIFICATION

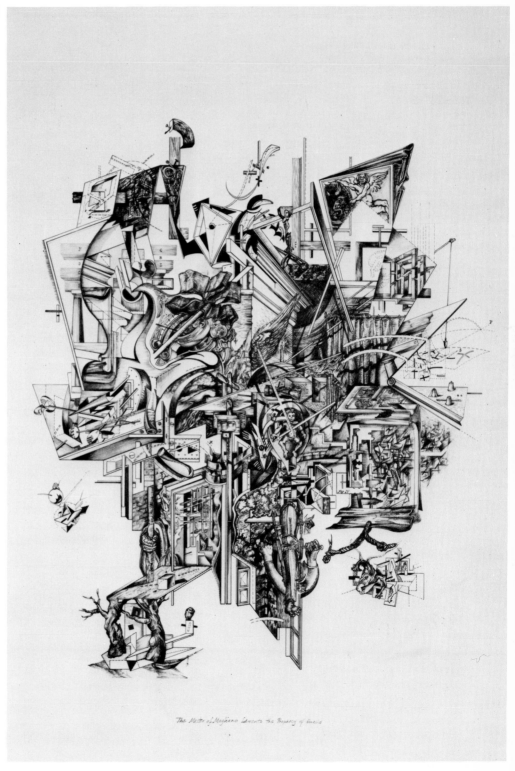

The Master of Mogliano Laments the Property of Rome